Freeing the Faith

Freeing the Faith

A Credible Christianity for Today

HUGH DAWES

First published in Great Britain 1992
SPCK
Holy Trinity Church
Marylebone Road
London NW1 4DU

British Library Cataloguing in Publication Data

A catalogue record for this book is
available from the British Library

ISBN 0-281-04580-1

Typeset by Pioneer Associates, Perthshire
Printed in Great Britain by
Mackays of Chatham plc.

Thankfully,
remembering my father, James,
for my mother,
for Malcolm
and for Christopher

Contents

Acknowledgements ix

Introduction 1

1 The failure of christian orthodoxy 4

2 A new story of God 21

3 The worth of humanity 38

4 Faith in life 54

5 Renewing the world 68

6 Valuing what is ordinary 83

7 An open church 96

8 Sufficient for the day 111

Notes 122

Index 127

Acknowledgements

I am grateful to many people for help given in many different ways in the writing of this book. Directly, it was Philip Law of SPCK who surprised me first of all with his suggestion that I might write it, but who has supported me since with much advice and thoughtful criticism – and with his patience too. Peter Walker, my former bishop, encouraged me with a gentle episcopal insistence to accept that invitation, at a time when I was anxious about the wisdom or possibility of doing so – one of many kindnesses I owe to him. And Leslie Houlden read the first draft of my manuscript and made valuable comments upon it. My personal debt to him, however, is far more than that. Like so many other Anglican clergy – and not all of them liberals! – I am grateful for the generosity of his teaching, support, friendship and encouragement over the years since I first knew him as my College Principal at Cuddesdon. If life in the Church of England can still at times seem fairly desperate, it would be far grimmer without his presence!

More obliquely, but no less really, I have been helped by the people I have worked with since being ordained. Philip Haynes, John Sturdy, Don Cupitt, Janet Phillips and Brigitte Snell have, as colleagues, been generous in time and talk and the sharing of ideas, and supportive in the stages of my own faith's development this far. That does not, of course, make them in any way responsible for, or implicated in, the views expressed here; but their companionship has meant a lot. So did that of the late Geoffrey Lampe and his wife Elizabeth, whom it was good briefly to know and love.

Ten years of my ministry have been spent working with students in Cambridge, at Gonville and Caius College and at Emmanuel College. Though christianity in a university can be even more depressingly conservative than in other settings, I was encouraged then by much serious and open discussion with young people in both colleges. They were places where it remained possible to be a priest to a whole community. If I had needed convincing that care, compassion and generous love are human qualities and not the preserve of the 'religious', that experience would have persuaded me.

Despite that background, however, this work really springs from pastoral rather than academic concerns. While life in a university strengthened my intellectual conviction as to the need for a liberal approach to faith, it has been in returning to parish ministry that I have grasped the full extent to which the language and concerns of traditional christianity no longer touch the basic realities of most people's lives. So my final thanks are properly to the people of the parish of St. James, Cambridge. To members of the church congregation here, first, for their kindness and tolerance of me and of my ideas. But even more to all those other people who are not churchgoers, whom I have come to know and whose stories I have tried to hear. For it is being with them, and wanting to take them seriously, which has required me to face the task of seeking to find some new way to tell this story – which sounds so foreign to them as to most others, but which can still mean so much to me.

Hugh Dawes
Cambridge, November 1991

Introduction

'Halt liberalism or become a sect' announced a headline in one of the church newspapers in the autumn of 1991, quoting a leading anglo-catholic layman and government minister, John Gummer. His was not the only voice coming out with such remarks at the time, and it seems unlikely that it will be the last. There is a lot of name-calling going on within mainstream christianity at present, and within the Church of England especially, and liberalism has been singled out as its target. The cry has gone up that the church is in danger, that its faith is under threat, and that the situation will only be resolved by either silencing the foe or else dividing churches in two. Liberalism, instead of being seen as an honourable position of tolerance and broad-mindedness, or something quite harmless even if rather 'wet', is now made out to be little short of the anti-Christ; 'the synthesis of all heresies' as Pope Pius X labelled Modernism in 1907, before proceeding to condemn and very efficiently ban it.

Recalling that earlier witch-hunt in the Roman Catholic church at the beginning of this century helps to get the present experience into perspective. Pius X in effect invented Modernism, treating it as a convenient religious dustbin into which to place a whole variety of ideas and approaches that were current then and of which he heartily disapproved – even (or especially!) when he failed to understand them. We see exactly the same thing happening now. Today's self-conscious traditionalists react against an enormous range of movements and changes within the church which they happen not to like. A host of quite separate matters earn their opprobrium: things as different – judging from the correspondence columns – as women's ordination, new service books, theological restatement and the reordering of church buildings! But all are crudely lumped together, one or two are sensationalized, and the whole package is labelled 'liberal' and hence untouchable. Dialogue is ruled out because there is held to be nothing to discuss. Religion is defined as being unchanging, so those who cannot accept that truth must go elsewhere.

This exclusivism is certainly not new in christianity, but the merest glance at the history of the churches makes plain its fallacy. For the self-same claims have been made down the centuries for many positions in both faith and practice. The shift and variety, the contest for what is held to matter, is actually what allows christianity to live. The traditionalists like to imagine that by purging the church of erroneous doctrine they will keep it pure and holy. Their fear of hearing conflicting voices, in the mistaken conviction that without them they will be free to concentrate on proclaiming timeless truth, seems in fact much more likely to make their 'traditional church' little more than an enclosed private club. Indeed, this is something that can be detected happening already in the 'continuing churches' of Anglican tradition in the United States. 'Halt liberalism *and* become a sect' would seem closer to the reality of the situation than Mr Gummer's wild claims. For the process of keeping oneself pure, once it has been embarked on in this way, is of course never ending. Before long someone, even in a traditional church, is likely to hear the voices of the wider world and not discount them as simply nonsense – and will promptly become the next 'liberal' requiring to be purged. The whole process is a way of decline and death.

This book, which is unashamedly an essay in liberal understanding, sees change and openness not as threatening to the christian faith, but as its chief hope.

Always looking back, as we know from the experience of trying to cross a busy road while having a conversation with someone else behind us, is a sure way to self-extinction. The religious point was brought home for me twenty years ago, when I first read some words that both startled and thrilled me at the end of an article by Dennis Nineham. With hindsight, I realize just how much they have remained with me since then, influencing my thinking and acting in any number of ways. Defending the role and importance of new christian thinking that was going on then, he made the point of the extent to which the New Testament portrait of Jesus was already problematic, as objective norm, less than 2,000 years after the event of his life. And he put this final question:

> What will be the case with the Christ of 2,000,000,000 years ago? That is a question theologians should not ignore, for we are quite credibly informed that the human race may yet have 2,000,000,000 years to go. When the Lord then comes will he find '*the* faith' on the earth? Do we really expect him to?[1]

That perspective surely gives the lie to the game the traditionalists want to play. It requires us all to recognize that even the most hallowed of formularies are provisional. It invites us to accept as both challenge and duty the job of setting faith free from tradition that merely tyrannizes, so that its voice can be heard afresh in the actual world of today.

1

The failure of christian orthodoxy

'My kingdom is not of this world,' the author of John's gospel has Jesus say to Pontius Pilate when they meet in the praetorium just before he is finally handed over to be crucified. The scene, in common with the whole of John's telling of the Passion – the story of the death of Jesus – is heavy in every kind of irony, far too much so for any of it to be treated naively as straightforward narrative or description. In this instance, what the words are struggling to express is the full ambivalence of a meeting here between political authority backed by military force and moral authority with no force beyond its own authenticity. Jesus does not dismiss the world that is Pilate's concern, so much as approach it from a different angle. Yet too many christians of a conservative background have preferred to ignore the irony in this. Instead the words have acquired for them a mistaken literalism, and so have become almost a talisman for self-styled traditionalist believers of every persuasion to justify the tragic irrelevance, by all the normal standards of our day, of the gospel they claim to uphold.

The bankruptcy of such a version of faith both intellectually and practically, the desperate need to replace it with one that is built upon the worth and importance of this world we inhabit, one that takes seriously the worldview of people today, is the central theme for this book. In the lifetime of Jesus, a large part of his persuasiveness for so many ordinary people appears to have been just such a moral credibility, the way he managed to throw light upon the real lives they

4

actually led. Yet this sort of being in touch that is so
evident in many of the gospel stories has today been all
but forgotten. Instead what we now hear, sometimes
explicitly, and implicitly many times more, is that the
church is not meant to speak the language of the world,
for the world is fallen and lost. It certainly wants to
address the world with its gospel of salvation, and
frequently in the most hysterical of ways, but the agenda
according to which this is done will be the church's
alone. On this understanding the christian message
belongs to a quite different realm of being, and is
necessarily therefore cast in a very different language
from that of the normal discourse of most men and
women. Christianity is taken to be at heart about the
promise of life *beyond* the material mode of our present
being; salvation is from the world rather than in it. In
the short term, and just for the time being, the role of the
church is to keep people safe and unharmed, cocooned
against the foes said to be lurking outside, until death
comes as the blessed release from all that threatens.

In many ways it is strange that such a creed can have
any followers at all. Yet clearly it has. Its appeal, if we
are honest, would seem to a great extent to be built on
that self-absorption and capacity for selfishness that is a
part of all human experience. Put crudely, it is the
ultimate hedging of bets to secure my survival should it
turn out that everyone else is destined to perish. It does
not appear to have any more than a superficial
connection with the willingness to set self aside and
concentrate on others which is again part of the gospel
portrait of the man Jesus. This may seem a hard
judgement in the light of the obvious accompanying
generosity of many traditional believers' lives, but that
alone is not sufficient to gainsay it. It is surely not
coincidence that in recent years fundamentalist and
born-again christianity has flourished in many settings
where the dicta of the free market economy and
individual greed have been accepted most uncritically.

This is apparent in Britain, in its 'yuppie' city congregations, and much more so in the United States, where a
strong lead along precisely these lines was given from
the White House during Ronald Reagan's time as
president.

Yet even with such backing the 'success' of what is on
offer remains very limited, certainly when viewed against
the background of a steady and today massive decline in
christian practice since the beginning of the nineteenth
century. It cannot mask the fact that, more generally,
christianity has lost touch with the lives of ordinary men
and women in the western world; that this faith that in
the past served to help fashion that world in so many
ways is now almost wholly marginalized within it. The
churches are certainly aware of this, as is evident from
so much talk and activity concerning mission within
them at the present time. Decades of evangelism in the
Anglican Communion, and of evangelization in the
Roman Catholic church, along with mission crusades of
various flavours in many countries, are all an indication
(however much we may personally despair of the
methods by which they operate) that people realize
something is amiss. We have lost our grip, and telling
'the old, old story' is not having the effect that it once
did.

We see the signs, yet we appear strangely incapable of
discerning what they are saying. Actual christian
perception of what this all means is so shallow because
believers – or certainly, it seems, the majority of religious
leaders – cannot get outside of the framework within
which the gospel appears quite 'OK' for them. Thus at
heart the only response being offered to people not
hearing is little more than shouting louder. Vast amounts
of time and energy are given over to what are matters of
presentation. For instance, the absence of young people
from christian congregations is noted and regretted, and
the solution to this is seen in terms of offering worship
and music that is more accessible to them, closer to the

style of the discotheque or wherever. The problem, in other words, is understood to be one simply of finding ways of *keeping* the young and others interested. It is essentially all about packaging; the actual product on offer remains unchanged since it is held as an article of faith that it is unchanging.

The point could be illustrated in any number of ways, but is certainly made very clear by looking at some of the christian hymns and songs produced in the last few years and considered to be modern. Shelf loads of volumes of these have appeared in the last twenty years or so, their covers bright, guitar chords added to the music, and even with instructions included in the pages of introduction about proper 'devotional' performance. Yet whatever the truth in claims to modernity so far as the music goes (and that is perhaps questionable!), the imagery of their texts is certainly something else. Ironically this is much closer to sixteenth-century ideas and thought than it is to today's world, or indeed to that of the hymns that were being written in Britain in the years between the first and second world wars. So for instance these words, from a hymn written in the 1970s with the refrain 'Our God reigns', immensely popular in charismatic christian circles and reckoned to be very modern and relevant there, might just as well have been written by Calvin in terms of their 'theology'. Indeed, so far as the whole of their imagery goes, they could come straight from the world of some of the New Testament writers:

> It was our sin and guilt that bruised and
>   wounded Him,
> It was our sin – that brought Him down.
> When we like sheep had gone astray, our
>   Shepherd came
> And on his shoulders – bore our shame.[1]

Such a verse, which is fairly typical of the genre, can be interestingly compared with hymns that were being written fifty or more years before. For instance, take the following lines written by Geoffrey Dearmer, which appear in the 1925 edition of *Songs of Praise*, a book that in its day was much used in schools and welcomed because of its approach – which was considered to be a much more open one than that of many 'church' books:

Where the many work together they with God
  himself abide,
But the lonely worker also finds him ever at his side.
Lo, the Prince of common welfare dwells within the
  market strife,
Lo, the bread of Heaven is broken in the sacrament
  of life.[2]

Certainly no one would want to claim that this hymn has not become dated – it is indeed quoted deliberately because it very much belongs to its times. Probably few would choose to sing it today, and it is certainly easy to criticize Dearmer's rhymes. Even so, what remains clear is that a genuine attempt has been made here to establish a link between the christian tradition and the circumstances of life at the time it was written, and indeed to rework the tradition in response to the particular insights and understandings of the time. It was precisely this sort of openness that alienated Dearmer, together with his brother Percy, from the anglo-catholic traditionalists they had previously been associated with. What must surely depress many about where we are now, and what speaks so very clearly about how far we have moved backwards, is that there is no hint whatever of any need being felt to do anything of this sort in the other, more recent, hymn, or in so many similar ones. Instead, it is simply assumed that you can apportion responsibility for the death of Jesus to worshippers who are living almost 2,000 years later – and treat this as something to sing about!

The same complaint of theological conservatism could be made with equal force about so much of the revision of liturgy in recent years, and even more about what has been claimed as the 'freeing' of worship in churches and congregations without any formal liturgical structure. Repeatedly, christians delude themselves into thinking that by activity of this sort they are responding to the problem, and that with a bit more effort they will surely bring the people *back*. Yet all the time they are doing nothing more than tinkering around. They completely miss the real point: which is that the majority, not only of the young but of all ages, are not interested in the least in what they see the church as having on offer; and that they have moved on light years ahead, and will never be brought back (they were never there anyway!) to the postures in which believers are set. Or perhaps christians *do* sense this, but are too frightened by what it might mean to look closer: that, regardless of wrappings, it is the goods on offer that in the light of today's understandings and awareness are so hopelessly flawed.

It is this, the monstrous irrelevance of what is termed christian 'orthodoxy', that so many practising believers find it impossible to grasp or appreciate. And the reason is surely that they have locked themselves into a private kingdom which is indeed 'not of this world'. Some christian commentators will even pride themselves on the fact that the gospel is of course only to be understood within the redeemed community and even there is not accessible to reason. Others, while not so extreme, still take for granted the situation in which faith has its own private language, and seemingly miss the point that until this changes radically, until it can be deeply and really grounded in the public language others speak, it renders true conversation and dialogue quite impossible. It simply does not occur to many christians to question ideas about the 'omnipotence' of God, the 'depravity' of human beings, a mechanism of 'redemption' which operates only through the shedding of a man's – Jesus' – blood, or a community possessed of 'eternal' truth given

once for all time. Even christian writers prepared to go
in for quite radical reinterpretations of many of the
terms persist in using them, despite the fact that the
new interpretation may well fly in the face of a word or
doctrine's original meaning! For all these things and
more are regarded by members of the church community
as the glories of their faith, and most cannot begin to
enter into the experience of all those outside for whom at
best such things are meaningless – and very often
frankly nonsensical. Those who are believers just do not
see the radical impossibility of traditional christianity
for large numbers of people, for we have cut ourselves
off from sharing their experience. Like Dickens's Miss
Havisham, we inhabit a world where time has stood
still. Since we ourselves do not notice the cobwebs and
decay that surround us, we have no chance of
understanding how these appear to others.

Instead, therefore, of facing squarely the indifference
that is shown towards the christian religion, and
examining what it might be within church life that
produces this attitude in others, what so often happens
is that members of the church become very angry about
this, and then take flight into fantasies that monstrously
distort and misrepresent what is actually happening. So
it is, for instance, that we frequently find in christian
congregations a great deal of talk about the church's
persecution, and of believers being required to suffer for
their faith. Such a perception of things, it has to be said,
is not peculiar to the christian religious tradition. In
contemporary Britain there is a precisely parallel type of
hysteria within the muslim community, most noticeable
in recent years concerning the publication of Salman
Rushdie's *The Satanic Verses*. But whether among
christians or muslims, the use in such circumstances of
the language of persecution is manifestly absurd. We
are here in the realms of 'newspeak', where words mean
whatever you want them to. A glance at the realities of
persecution in either religious tradition, in the past or in

other parts of the world more recently, will quickly make this plain. Christians are not genuinely persecuted in Britain or anywhere else in Europe nowadays, certainly not since the liberalization that has taken place in the countries of the former communist bloc. They may indeed sometimes be laughed at – but then so may stamp collectors, or bird twitchers, or any other group of enthusiasts within society more generally. The difference is that most other groupings can accept this in good humour.

For an enthusiasts' group is exactly what the church has now by and large become. Religion has ceased to be a dimension in the natural, everyday life of most people, and has become instead something private, a club for those who like it. This is the reality of how things are, whatever claims may still angrily be made that everyone *ought* to like it. As a private club, separated from the generality of society, christianity cannot expect to be exempt from that bemusement, at times extending further into amusement, which all such groupings provoke. But christians have no more right to speak of their persecution than do the members of a London gentlemen's club! Doing so just reinforces the view that they do not merit any sort of serious treatment.

Such alienation, for that is what we are really talking about and what has overtaken the church through its separation from the lives of the majority, is of course self-generating. As it increases it becomes necessary both to explain it – hence the distortion in the use of language we have observed – and then to justify it. So it leads with an apparent inevitability, through the impulse of this second requirement, to that exclusivism which is such a depressing feature of the present christian scene. Churches take to looking in on themselves, and at least metaphorically closing their doors in case it becomes too obvious how very few there are about with any sort of desire to come in. Perversely, as we have seen in terms of the mission activity touched on above and now becoming so prominent, the claim is still made that they want members and that the gospel is there for all. Yet in practice this can only ever come about provided it is according to their own narrow, prescriptive terms.

Within the Church of England the process is seen very clearly, and its consequences become sickeningly apparent, in the attitudes taken towards infant baptism. Anglicanism's foundation documents, its history and its current canon law all make plain that the church professes to baptize children without exception or qualification. The sacrament, the christening service, is understood to be a sign of divine generosity and love for all – a most appropriate sign therefore to match the joy of so many parents, the sense of gratitude for life and new life, that is part of the birth of a child. If parents want it, they should surely have it. The church bestows baptism in terms of its own faith. It does not require that a child's parents be themselves churchgoers or card-carrying christians before they can approach it.

More and more, however, the christening of babies nowadays is something done grudgingly, or only if parents are prepared to jump through a series of theological hoops, or else is not done at all. Families are fobbed off instead with pathetic substitutes – *The Alternative Service Book* contains a feeble, half-baked service of 'Thanksgiving for the Birth of a Child' – which, where they are used, frequently become yet another occasion for a clergyman or clergywoman to get at people not involved in the church's life, instead of serving as an opportunity to rejoice with them. One of the cupboards in the church where I work is still stuffed with leaflets previously used to push this 'Thanksgiving' service to parents who came seeking their child's baptism. This service, they were told, is for those who are not 'sure about Christian belief', since it does not ask them to 'promise to be faithful in Church going nor do they make vows publicly that they are Christian disciples'. Child baptism is strictly for the nobs, reserved for the offspring of those who 'will need to Pray, go to Church and be committed Christian disciples'.

The leaflet, and the approach that lies behind it, assumes a very clear distinction between the christian community and the rest of humanity. It puts the emphasis on a literal understanding of the spoken formularies in the baptism service – which do indeed appear to polarize church and world, light and darkness – and insists that these can be said only if 'taken seriously'. They are regarded as plain statements of fact, not poetic imagery that might be uttered in a little more relaxed manner. Whereas liberal christians want to see that second understanding made more explicit in any future reworking of the rites of baptism, the traditionalists' approach is the exact opposite. The 'public' view of baptism as a this-worldly rite of passage for birth is scorned in favour of a narrow church view which insists on seeing it as initiation into a separate community, a rite of passage *between* worlds – the lost and the redeemed. And the effect of this is that what might be a key setting in which it would be possible to discover common ground between church and community, one where the 'club' could be seen not as alien but as fully human like everyone else, becomes just another demonstration of christianity's separation and foreignness. It would be laughable, were it not so tragic, that the leaflet I have quoted carries on its back page an injunction to those who had to be content with the 'Thanksgiving' service – 'do not feel rejected'. We know we are kicking you in the teeth, but we hope it will not hurt![3]

Something similar can be seen happening with regard to Anglican practice on marriages, again in spite of its own formularies and its – and in this case the nation's – law. In England people have a legal right to be married in the church of the parish in which they are resident, irrespective of religious profession or its absence. Yet in many parishes more and more couples are being told that this is not the case, or are not told that it is, and are led to believe that 'christian marriage' is something reserved for christian believers. The ease with which this can be said and done reflects a change at a still deeper level, in terms of the widespread abandonment of what has hitherto been the foundation for the understanding of how Anglican ministry works – the parish system.

The church, on this ancient model, belongs to a place, to a whole community, rather than to a gathered congregation. It is the religious expression of that community's life for everyone, regardless of whether people are believers or unbelievers, churchgoers or not. Generous in its understanding, it gladly offers provision for the 'hatching, matching and dispatching' of all within its boundaries. The ordained person is a priest for everyone in the parish, not the private minister to the gathered congregation. But this latter role is the one that many more of those being ordained now want to occupy, not least because it is frequently the only pattern of ministry they have themselves experienced. Because, in cities particularly, it is increasingly the case that christians worship in the church whose flavour suits them rather than that of the community where they live, it is all too easy for the genuine, parish-wide care and concern to be dropped. Members of the congregation will not notice this and, even if they did, many might not be much bothered about it. So we can see how it is that with weddings also a point of possible contact with people, a pastoral opportunity capable of demonstrating that the church shares in the spontaneous joys of ordinary people's lives, is sacrificed on the altar of ritual purity.[4] Just when society generally has begun once again to put value on community, the church on the ground – by its actions if not in its words, for certainly much has recently been written within the Church of England on the importance of community to our lives[5] – seems ready to let it go.

Other areas of christian life and practice reveal the

same 'touch me not' approach, the same preference for apartness rather than anything that might run the risk of contamination by the world. We see a shrinking of vision, not least when it comes to matters of ethics and morality. In the nineteenth century, whatever brickbats it may be possible to throw at the ambiguous subject of Victorian morality, it was still the case that in many areas of life – for instance public health, people's working conditions, prison reform, slavery – christians were actively involved as advocates of, and also agents for, change.[6] Within the resources of the tradition were found ideas and strands capable of development to countenance and advance change in many areas, and this opportunity was made good use of. Today, across a wide range of issues, the tradition is approached and used quite differently, and chiefly in order to say 'no'. So on matters such as abortion, IVF, attitudes to homosexuality, or even something so apparently uncontroversial as equal status and opportunities for women, those who set themselves up as christian representatives appear frequently to stand against the possibilities of change in understanding which many in the wider society are concerned for and anxious to see. Sometimes, indeed, there may be valid grounds for 'holding the line' on a particular subject. But all too often the christian response to anything appears to be a knee-jerk reaction of intransigence – the world out there is wrong! – whatever it is that is being discussed. And increasingly the consequence of this is that whereas once christians were creatively involved in ethical debates, were seen to be so, and were appreciated and known to be so, now they are frequently left out because they are considered to have nothing useful to contribute. The dearth of moral theologians in the Church of England is one small sign of this, but in terms of any future reversal of the situation is a particularly depressing one. The death-wish of exclusivism has its effect.

The same forces that seek to reject the world outside

are also very much active and at work when it comes to life *within* the church. For if it is a major duty of believers to repel contamination from outside, it is also clearly vital that purity be maintained inside. More and more therefore (even if similar processes have undoubtedly operated within christianity in previous periods), christians who do not toe the line of rigid 'orthodoxy', those who ask questions and may even suggest that things need to change, are dismissed out of hand as heretics. The process has been particularly evident in the Roman Catholic church during the pontificate of John Paul II,[7] but is not restricted to that church alone. Within the Church of England attacks made upon the Bishop of Durham during the 1980s, questioning his right to function as a bishop, are very much signs of the times. The church's view on this as on so much else seems hopelessly blinkered. In terms of the extent of the alienation of most people in Britain from the tenets and worldview of christianity, David Jenkins's calls for reassessment and restatement are hardly earth-shattering, and certainly not dangerously liberal. To read, for example, some of the Easter sermons preached in his cathedral which have so outraged conservative christians each year is indeed to come into contact with a questioning mind, and a mind that is willing to ask whether the resurrection of Jesus need necessarily be tied to accounts of resurrection phenomena, and in particular that of the empty tomb. Yet it is a mind firmly convinced none the less of there being a reality to resurrection.[8] For today's neo-conservatives though, that will not do. Christianity for them is a total package, delivered once and for all and incapable of change, and you must either take or leave the whole. No compromise with uncertainty is allowed. So once again the consequence is that many more open believers, certainly those in situations where they feel themselves surrounded by sniping conservatives, back off in despair, realizing that they are not welcome. Narrowness results in a further retreat, the true tragedy of which is not able to be perceived by those whose actions bring it about.

This process of self-willed decline is what I mean when I speak of the failure of 'orthodoxy'. Has it now become quite unstoppable? At least some open, liberal believers want to challenge it and consider it worth trying, as I personally discovered from the letters I received in response to an article questioning whether a liberal understanding of faith was nowadays something it was impossible for Anglicans to maintain.[9] Because liberalism by its nature is open, cautious and questioning, because one of its main tenets is the desire to include rather than cast out, its adherents have for too long refrained from challenging openly the position of conservatives. Though the latter are frequently complaining that the management of the Church of England is in the grip of the liberals, it is certainly not the case that this 'control' shows when it comes to christianity's public face. The conservatives have been allowed to get away with the pretence that their version of faith, and their view of the church as a body set apart, is the only true christianity, and also the way it has always been. Meanwhile, those with a more open understanding have for whatever reason been prepared to suffer without complaining the decline and alienation that has followed from allowing the conservatives to hold the centre of the religious stage. Thus tarred with 'orthodoxy's' brush, liberals have in consequence all but disappeared from view. And so the possibility that christianity might exist in a form that related to reason and to the world people inhabit has effectively been lost sight of.

But the point has now been reached where it is vital to do battle and to protest. Liberals need to denounce what passes for orthodoxy and stand clearly apart from it. For the claims the 'orthodox' make for themselves and their ideas are nonsense. Though christians in the first two centuries did speak of themselves as aliens in the world, that world was something of which, at a deeper level, they were none the less very much part. Subsequently, and convincingly after Constantine became Roman emperor, the sense of being aliens vanished, and was recognized to be much more a feature of a particular period of the church's history than a distinctive or permanent aspect to christian consciousness. The idea today that there is merit in the church being a wholly isolated community, distanced in its spiritual purity from the wider world, guarding and enclosing truth that owes nothing whatsoever to that world, is something very recent, and owes more to a particular view of the circumstances of our day than it does to any constant in christian history. Before its appearance, and despite its claim, christianity has always been formed and shaped, in part at least, by the world in which it has been set, and by the ideas, imagery and concerns of that world. The relationship between the two is a dynamic one, and one capable of immense creativity and benefit in both directions. It is not anything forced, not an imposing of the patterns and ideas of a wicked world on to the church, so contaminating its doctrinal purity. That claim is a distortion and lie that has to be unmasked. For, as Wayne Meeks has well written with regard to the first christian communities in the New Testament period, 'those patterns were part of themselves, part of who they were, how they thought and how they felt'.[10] Whatever differences there may have been in the past between christian believers and others within the wider society, they still inhabited the same world and shared most basic perceptions of it. That was precisely what made discourse possible, and so allowed the rapid growth of the christian movement in those years. Even when christians were anxious to profess their distinctiveness this was still, as Meeks makes very clear, *within* a world to which they fully belonged:

> For example, Paul wrote, 'Do not be conformed to this world, but be transformed by the renewal of your

minds' (Rom. 12.2). Yet his typical admonitions, which follow those words, are sprinkled with topics and turns of phrase that would be instantly recognizable in the moral rhetoric of his time and place. The Christians whose moral formation we are trying to understand lived in the world of the early Roman empire, and that world also lived in them: in their thinking, in their language, in their relationships.[11]

Just such a recognition that we *belong* to our present world, and a willingness to reinterpret the christian faith in terms of that world's thinking and understandings, is what is required of the church now if it is to continue in any real way to inform (as well as itself being informed by) the world outside of the church. Otherwise christianity is bound to become – as in so many settings it already appears to be – just another sect, another private universe reserved solely for those who wish to abandon the wider world of their fellow women and men. Doubtless it can survive as such, in the same way that Jehovah's Witnesses and others survive, but the price paid will be the forfeiting of any true claim to relate outside of its boundaries. Such an inability to connect with the world outside of itself might reassure some with the knowledge of their doctrinal purity, but it would actually make the church a wholly different animal from what it has been in previous times.

Because christians have for too long prevaricated over incorporating new knowledge and understanding into faith's expression, the degree of adjustment that is now required is bound to be very painful for many. For those who have been brought up on certainties and assurances, the openness required by a liberal understanding, the degree of restatement it is going to demand, is inevitably frightening and may well appear brutally iconoclastic. As we shall see in the chapters that follow, great structures are in need of tearing down, for the simple

reason that nothing more can be done with them. Much
that people have gone on reciting, claiming and
professing has in reality died and, if there is to be any
possibility of 'resurrection', that death now has to be
faced squarely and can no longer be backed away from.

> We cannot revive old factions
> We cannot restore old policies
> Or follow an antique drum.[12]

Accepting that 'the old, old story' will not be told
again as it was before is for many anything but easy. Yet
if only it can be faced, people may quickly find that great
burdens are indeed lifted and great release felt. And at
the same time whole new opportunities will be seen to
open up, as much as for those who are 'within' the
church community as for others who at present look on
bemused. For to recover the possibility of religion as a
part of life, natural, normal, everyday, uniting people
rather than separating them off, does lead to the
discovery of a continuity with earlier christian experience
at a level that goes genuinely deeper than that of
doctrines and formularies. Accepting that we do not
believe the same things as they did then actually frees us
to *relate* again, both to the world and to that which we
name as God, as they in their time were able to. Once we
do that, faith too is freed, and can begin to live again.

2

A new story of God

At one level, relating to the world is something the church cannot help but do, whether it wishes to or not. A religion that is made up of people is bound to do this in some sense, for the plain fact that we share one humanity, that we are creatures of the same species, ensures that we have some relationship with one another. The most exclusive religious sect, and the solitary hermit with an individual creed of his own, do in spite of themselves show that they relate with others in the world, even if it is only by their decision *not* to relate! The real issue then is whether christianity now has the courage and faith to relearn and renew this relationship, to retell its story creatively so that it can not only be heard, but be felt to matter. For many centuries of the church's history (though perhaps not during the first few decades of its life), even to suggest such a thing openly would have seemed wrong. For the world was 'given', and people's places in it were fixed. Religious truth was something *handed down* to men (to men exclusively, who then in turn would have passed on such parts as they felt appropriate to their women, children and slaves). God or the gods made themselves known to the extent that this was appropriate for a subject humanity.

This theory predates christianity. It was taken over fairly uncritically from the church's jewish parent – with embellishments of its own being added before long – quite soon after the death of Jesus. The new religion, as it grew, set about working it out in a variety of ways; in understandings, for instance, of human authority under

21

God in both church and state, and of the weighty significance that should be afforded to christian tradition. But it came eventually to be most clearly enshrined (and this can be seen today within both catholic and protestant traditions of christianity) in a view of 'scripture' – its sacred writings; this, even though the full-bloodedness of the position arrived at would probably have surprised many of the authors of the actual texts thus set up and exalted. This under-standing, which is still very much in evidence and expressed most clearly – though certainly not solely – by those who are happy with the title of biblical funda-mentalists, asserts that it is God, rather than any human 'intermediaries', who is the true author of scripture. God uses this means to communicate to human beings all that they need to know, and that he wants them to know, about religious truth. If they only conform themselves to it they can come to no harm. This conviction we find stated very plainly by a leading Anglican evangelical, James Packer:

> . . . the Bible writers unanimously and unambiguously testify to a God who *speaks*, in the straightforward sense of that word – that is, a God who addresses verbal messages to people, states facts, tells us things; and therefore evangelicals affirm, on the basis of the Bible literally interpreted, that cognitive instruction via Scripture is integral to God's self-disclosure and that biblical teaching, as such, is God's teaching, as such.[1]

This view is evidently one that remains attractive to a good many believers. Yet it will not do if we genuinely want the christian story to live again. For the average person outside of the church (and indeed for more and more who are within its ranks), claims of this sort simply do not make sense, and a faith community that just goes on asserting them is indeed beyond compre-hension. To be sure, there are problems, as we shall be seeing later on, with much of the content of what is claimed to be given in this way. But the incredulity starts here, with the whole notion that we can appeal outside or beyond ourselves for our knowledge and understanding.

Nowadays we know a great deal about how human beings actually organize themselves: that they do so, for instance, by their own conscious decision, and that they formulate the rules and then determine both who is in and who is out. We know this to be how it is whether the organization concerned is one at the level of club, local community, nation state, or wherever. Sociological method has allowed us to see the processes at work, so that we understand clearly the fact of the human investment in this, but also recognize the quite regular desire of people in so many spheres to claim a 'higher' authority for what they are doing than their own decision alone. And when it comes to other, rival faith traditions, christians certainly seem quite happy to recognize that religion is no exception to this. People create religion too in order to give some sense to their experience of life in the world. Only when that task is begun do they, as part of the process, invoke the approval of the gods to validate what they have already done.

Traditionalist christians gladly accept this, as I have said, with regard to other faiths, because it fits with their insistence that the gods of other faiths are false. But this is indeed to want to have one's cake and eat it. The recognition that the formulation of faith and of religion is a human activity of this kind is something we now have to see that christianity cannot be immune from. The claims that are made that it is otherwise lack any agreed external, neutral or unbiased authority to which they can appeal. They are all christian assertions from within. And while this may not of itself require that they be false, it certainly does mean that they are placed on precisely the same footing as the essentially identical claims, religious or otherwise, made by any

other group of human beings. For each alleges that a
monopoly of truth belongs to its own understanding. In
the religious area many try to reinforce this with the
idea that this truth has been given from above, while
both within and outside of religion the role of the revered
human teacher never to be surpassed is made much of.

Now, we must indeed allow that it does not necessarily
follow from this that christian assertions of such a
monopoly of truth are nonsense. This might be – as
traditional believers have wanted to maintain – the
single exception to the norm. But any such continued
claim is certainly not helped by the fact that so much
with which it is bound up *is* nonsense, and that a great
deal of it has been known to be so for a long time. Open,
liberal exploration of the christian tradition itself has a
long history now, and has produced its results. In the
nineteenth century the combined effect of scientific
discovery and of biblical criticism managed to complete
a process that had been going on for some 300 years,
and finally destroyed not just the previously allegedly
historical account of the universe as something fixed
and certain which most church people derived from the
bible, but also undermined – and in the long run this
would be much more significant – the whole notion that
that account, or anything else, could be authoritative
and binding for all time. Truth was something that
human beings were in a constant process of discovering
for themselves – not something you could claim at any
point in time to have been given once for all. The bible
was no exception to this, and so it ceased, at least in any
straightforward sense, to be the word of God which
tradition had claimed. Its human authors could be
discerned, and their own interests, concerns and
situations identified. You could see *how* these affected
what they wrote, and you could see that it was *they* who
wrote, not God leaving messages on a dictaphone.
Biblical writers all had their own goals and, when these

required it, could even be less than honest just like everyone else.

Superficially, nowadays even most conservative christians would have to accept the truth of some of this. Few would any longer make claims that Moses wrote the whole of the Pentateuch (the first five books of the Old Testament) or King David penned all of the Psalms. Yet at the time when these myths were first shattered, the violence of reaction was no less than when gentle liberals today attempt to recast the idea of resurrection. And for the same reason. The foundations (to borrow Paul Tillich's splendid phrase) appeared to be shaking, and it was the whole notion of authority that quite rightly was seen to be threatened. Since christianity had appeared to be built on precisely these concepts of authority, many were desperate to hold the line. So throughout the nineteenth century we see liberals being attacked in all branches of christianity, not least within the Roman Catholic church. If Protestants most felt the hurt of critical knowledge applied to scripture, Catholics soon found that the idea of an unchanging tradition given by God was no more immune to historical scrutiny than an infallible bible. John Henry Newman, though so cautious and conservative in many respects, recognized this when he talked of the *development* of doctrine. 'To live is to change', Newman said, and survived doing so to become a cardinal, even though he was highly suspect to many. Within a few years, however, George Tyrrell – like Newman also a convert from Anglicanism – would carry such ideas considerably further. Tyrrell talked of an authority that was diffused rather than focused. 'Supreme authority', he wrote, 'rests with the *whole* church and not with Rome.' God has no direct and infallible hot-line to us. Rather, God relates to men and women 'by the gradual evolution of his mind and will in the collective spirit of mankind'.[2]

In many ways I believe that Tyrrell anticipated a

great deal of what open christians are seeking to say today. But the violence of opposition that he experienced was a world apart from that which his liberal successors still face, whatever may be felt in the 1990s about the methods of a conservative papacy or may have to be endured because of them. Tyrrell was silenced and, when he refused to heed the ban, was excommunicated and forbidden to function as a priest. When he died, and had to be buried in an Anglican cemetery since he was excommunicate, even the friend who said a requiem mass for him found himself within a week suspended universally from functioning as a priest. For Tyrrell's liberalism was labelled as 'Modernism', a system in a sense constructed by the then pope, Pius X, simply in order to be condemned.[3]

If past experiences of that sort are to be regarded as precedents, things would hardly appear encouraging for those with a desire to renew christian believing today! Yet the real situation is now very different. Up until the last century and (despite all the speed in the advances of knowledge) still to a considerable extent during it, the new learning was having to do battle, within the church and outside, with a consensus of understanding that had itself been set by traditional christianity. Religion had fixed the rules of the game with its assertion that all were actually fixed by God. But that is no longer so. Nowadays the claims that are made for 'revelation', the technical term used for the giving of truth from above, must fly in the face of the generality of human knowledge. The more honest traditionalists acknowledge this, even though they then try to make a virtue of it. So they will claim that faith is above reason and inaccessible to reason. The true believer will not be bound by 'the wisdom of this world'.[4] The renaissance of this kind of thinking in the late twentieth century owes much to the theological system devised in the 1930s by the German theologian Karl Barth. But it chooses to ignore the extent to which Barth's thought was itself the product of his historical situation, with his desire to be able to assert a higher authority than Nazism. Its advocates miss the irony of a system designed to resist the tyrannies of the thought police of Hitler's Germany becoming similarly tyrannous itself, with ultimate authority handed over this time to allegedly incontrovertible scripture.

The Paul whom Barth tried to claim as his inspiration was fully aware, as we have seen already, of the world's wisdom, made use of it, and fashioned his thoughts within it. The conviction for others of the gospel he preached was built upon this. Open and liberal believers can therefore claim Paul in this particular sense as their ally when, in today's world, they let go of these ideas of revelation and of hot-lines to eternal truth, and instead say straightforwardly that christian faith is a wholly human work. Traditionalists will of course bleat about the abandonment of what has been 'given'; but the consequences of christianity's inability, thus far, to recast itself in line with the rest of contemporary knowledge in our day is plain to see in its steady decline throughout this century. Plain enough, surely, to suggest that we have to start again.

It is not, to be sure, that the church is actively disliked in the contemporary western world, certainly not in present-day Britain. In many areas an ordained person like myself will still encounter much friendship and goodwill from the people in the area where he or she works. They will talk about the good that the church does and, in a variety of ways from supporting its jumble sales to helping to keep its roof on, show that they value its presence and something of what it stands for. When they are allowed to they will still seek to come to it for ceremonies to mark the turning points of life. What they will not feel able to do, however, is join in its regular pattern of worship. 'I do believe in God, but I don't go to church.' That familiar statement is more than the expression of complacency or indifference that churchgoers often dismiss it as. It encodes a great deal. Above all, I believe, it speaks of the inability of so many to accept what appears as the central tenet of the private world christians generally inhabit. It indicates to us their distance from what they assume *believing in God* must mean, when read off from the church's public face.

'I do believe in God, but . . .' What most people do not any longer believe in is the celestial controller giving wisdom from above to which christianity's language still appears always to point. They might not articulate it so sharply, but their gut instincts are clear. The universe is indeed a blend of 'chance and necessity',[5] and the notion of a God who pulls the strings to control it (or the subtle variant of a God who could do this, but chooses not to) has died. This 'god' that people cannot believe in, the fixed point apparently for traditionalists in the christian faith, has been defined very precisely by Richard Swinburne: 'a person without a body (i.e. a spirit) who is eternal, free, able to do anything, knows everything, is perfectly good, is the proper object of human worship and obedience, the creator and sustainer of the universe'.[6]

That people have left behind belief in that sort of a God is a fact not gainsaid by the existence of a few pious leftovers. Traditionalists sometimes stake a lot on the evidence opinion polls and surveys provide for the survival of prayer. And as a priest I am indeed sometimes asked by those I meet at the bus stop or the shops to pray about things or people for them. But it seems clear to me that they really do not expect that any magical change or resolving of circumstances will follow from words uttered into the void. That understanding is just something to joke about, as evidenced by the rather more frequent quips to me as to what I have been doing to produce a spell of particularly bad weather. A request for prayer from people outside the church community is much more a statement about something mattering to the person who has asked, and an awareness of the priest as someone who gives time to things that matter. It certainly does not involve *them* in subscribing to the sort of cosmology that first gave rise to the practice of prayer, the church's continuing belief in which, as they imagine, is a big part of what separates them from christianity. So while the church may pray for them, and in a strange way people will value this, they would not wish to be involved themselves in the mumbo-jumbo or the superstition which, apparently for mainline believers, still stands at the heart of this.

An open christianity seeking genuinely to renew the religious dimension to life needs first of all therefore, and unambiguously, to set about recasting the myth or the story of God. Christian origins lay in a world that was 'full of gods'. This was something the new faith could presume and work with. In the New Testament, the author of the Book of Acts shows Paul doing just this in the story of his preaching in Athens, a story that demonstrates the cosmological restraint of christianity – shared with judaism – when compared with other traditions at that time. The 'unknown god' who was just one in the Athenian pantheon is in fact the only God there is.[7] The idea of rivalry between supreme beings is rejected as superstition by both judaism and christianity, even if in the New Testament period the belief still remained that there were other, lesser, supernatural orders. Similarly, the christian ascription of divine attributes to the human figure of Jesus marked a further enormous shift in religious understanding, the true radicalism of which subsequent christian formulations very quickly backed away from. We see many of the church fathers preferring to stress what they claim as Jesus' predominant 'divinity', rather than give much attention to his genuine humanity.

Yet even with those formularies, and orthodoxy's often ferocious activities on their behalf, that world full of gods, that second spiritual universe, has continued to shrink steadily as time has gone by. Whatever might still be claimed for God, the accompaniments – the array of spirits good and bad, and a devil as personal as God – have generally collapsed in spite of the formularies. Christians may say Sunday by Sunday that they join in worship in the eucharistic prayer 'with angels and archangels, and with all the company of heaven', but for most of them nowadays this is more a part of the poetry of faith than any statement of literal fact. Save in those extreme fundamentalist circles that take delight in dredging up the detritus from the christian rubbish heap, God is the only 'other' for those in the mainstream of traditional christian belief today.

If christians are to justify and make good the claim that the story of God has significance for people still, we shall need not only to own up to that, but to push our rethinking quite a bit further. For just what is this 'other' that we claim we are speaking of? Some will say indignantly that the question is invalid, that we cannot penetrate beyond this point. God, for them, is what lies behind all the human formulations, inaccessible to the naming process of language by which human beings define, and order, and even 'create'. But that simply will not do. The notion of 'God' contained within Swinburne's definition which I quoted is not a given, but is itself part of the formulation, and every bit as much a human work as anything else. Nowadays we are able to see how it emerged, and understand how it could, within the jewish–christian tradition, in that hierarchical and pyramidical society which existed at the time of the monarchy begun by King David. As on earth, so also in heaven. The pyramid must continue upwards, with God at the top of it. This was also a society, as so many Old Testament stories make plain, in which power was all important, and where the powerful considered them-selves the only ones capable (normally deferring, of course, to God!) of bringing anything into being. So ultimate power, power in its highest form, could not help but belong to God, and God must surely be the final source of everything that is, and of how it is, and things that happen must do so positively and deliberately because of God. And then finally this was a society and culture in which, as in so many others at the time, ideals were generally personified in order to be understood. God then would have to be like a person if what God expressed was to ring true.

But that world is not our world at all. So that formulation must now be replaced if we are to breathe life into what it once spoke of. Far too much energy has been expended by christian writers in recent years in trying to keep alive the portrait of the personal and omnipotent God despite all the evidence to the contrary. Rather than accept that experiences like the holocaust, or our human devising of gruesome new weapons of destruction (quite apart from our extensive new knowledge of the world), have rendered the idea of such a God meaningless, christians instead have struggled in a whole variety of ways to somehow try and rescue the notion. There has been the claim, for instance, that God *allows* freedom to human beings, albeit at the price of his own and others' hurt.[8] Yet all of the loving care and insight with which much of this writing and thinking has been done does not alter the fact that it has really been energy wasted. People tie themselves in knots to prove that divine omnipotence need not mean quite what it seems, rather than face the fact that it was a myth which no longer works and now must be honestly let go of.

Only dare to do that, however, and then we can begin afresh. Admitting that the ideas of divine personhood and a heavenly hierarchy have served their time and no longer work, we gain the freedom to find new words for God. The starting point for this is there clearly enough in that fundamental christian perception that we have already noted, that God was seen and known in a human life in Jesus. Heaven, in other words, and all that accompanies it, has come down to earth once and for all.

So rather than 'stand looking up toward heaven',[9] condemning religious language for all time to speaking of a fantasy realm inhabited by human beings writ large, up-market versions of hobgoblins and all the characters from Narnia, we can say clearly that the christian religion has to do with the depths that are present *within* life. Even then, believing in God is going to require a sustained act of faith when we take note of the cynicism and despair that feature so much today. But it is at least a credible faith, in the sense that it genuinely starts from where we are now.

To talk about God is quite simply to talk about life having the capacity for meaning and purpose. In no way can these ever simply be the property of believers. The meaning and purpose are there potentially in every life, whether or not people recognize them or choose to respond. In that sense, as the christian tradition maintains, God always is. Even so, acknowledging that there is this dimension to our existence is clearly going to affect us. We may not want to say that it 'saves' us, in the narrow sense in which that word has so often been used within christianity (salvation being the rescuing of individuals, with the implication that others are lost), but it clearly does give to the lives of many of those who have glimpsed it a conscious, deliberate involvement in what it is felt to be about. Understood like that it may indeed be said to save, since it presents people with a sense of meaning and purpose that challenges the destructive forces that are also so evident in life. More than that, it generates a commitment in us, moving us so that we seek to co-operate with it and want to further it. Stripped of the make-believe of omnipotence, the meaning and purpose of God are things to be worked at in the company of others if they are to be achieved. The meaning offered to us is also the meaning we must make real.

If we are wanting to spell out what constitutes this meaning we need first to recognize, however strange it may seem from the more traditional perspective, that its expression is always provisional. It is not unitary, fixed, the same for all time, but has always to be worked out, in a particular circumstance or setting, through the experience of a community or in the life of an individual within it. It is constantly upsetting notions of what is given, precisely because it responds to realities in this way. But within that movement, certain themes weave themselves and play a part. All of them are things earthed in the christian tradition, though at a level deeper than that of a surface assenting to creeds or doctrines: love, most obviously, but along with it peace, justice, compassion, truth and moral goodness. And beauty also, I would want to claim, as something deeper and more all-embracing than the physical attractiveness that we so often limit it to. All these strands are ones that can be traced to, and focus naturally around, the figure of Jesus as much of the christian tradition has communicated him to us. So too is the provisionality of which they are part; Jesus the 'saboteur of received ideas'[10] breaks open the mould of any established order. Yet it is important to say – vitally important if christianity is to be seen as a real faith possibility for today – that these things are not bound to the figure of Jesus alone. They will also find a focus both in the experiences of human life together and, for many people, around moments in their own lives when, even if only for a short while, the picture has seemed to come together and they have felt things to be whole and true. Such moments, the particular experience, may well be fragile and may quickly pass; yet that should not cause us to doubt that they have happened, or to think ourselves unchanged by them.

For a delicate understatement of just such an experience, we could well look to a poem by William Plomer called 'Reading in the Garden'. The poet sits on an August day, trying to summon some enthusiasm for two books (one by Tanner and the other by Lucinda) that he must review, but is sharply aware of his surroundings, of his own life experience, and of the ambiguity of the world in which all are set:

> It is not easy to be calm as if
> The air we breathe were not corrupt,
> Not full of the dirty floating
> Corrosive filaments of hate and lies.
>
> All the same, I am conscious of privilege,
> Of being sustained by stress and effort
> Over a long time, by many,
> And so brought to this place,
>
> This after-midway moment.
> So, with a sense of obligation
> I take up and open
> A book – never mind which.
>
> Oh, but this minimal, ephemeral
> Insect speeding on the page –
> What a risk! How very precarious
> To be it, here, now!
>
> Whether the book is Tanner's or Lucinda's
> A turn of the page would blot it out:
> Impermanence we have in common –
> We have life too.
>
> The music of a huge joy swells,
> Rises, floods my veins and bones,
> And the fine nerves of my skin tingle:
> This is life, it feels like hope.[11]

The fragility there of an insect on a page triggers a profound awareness of things that none the less matter – 'The music of a huge joy. . . . This is life, it feels like hope.' Of such moments people will say often that they have been touched, and touched by something that is real. Even if we shrug our shoulders, blink hard, get back to whatever task was in hand, we are in some sense changed by such experiences, and the response we make to the world subsequently is likely to be different, whether consciously or not.

Wherever, whenever women and men know experiences of this kind – and they happen in a whole variety of ways, ways that are natural and not magically induced – it is a religious experience. Very often christianity has been reluctant to allow this, for part of its exclusivism has been its determination to keep all true religion to itself, and so restrict access to God strictly to those who knock at its door. But any future, open christianity will tread a quite different path on such matters. It will want to respond positively to such aspects of everyday life, affirming that they do indeed matter as people sense in themselves that they do. It will see its task as being to welcome them and, where necessary, point to their significance, rather than either dismiss them according to the criteria of some version of orthodoxy, or else try to explain them and squeeze them into orthodoxy's mould. Love and compassion, insight into the preciousness and marvel of life, do actually mean something to people. If they could only be treated sensitively by the members of a community of faith, then that might begin to open up the language of God to all those others who know them. Persistence, on the other hand, with the portrait of one who as Judge is said to require the death of miserable sinners is unlikely to touch many where they are, other than those who are inwardly – for whatever reason – deeply disturbed. Too often in the past christianity has actually contributed to people's mental hurt. Liberal believers must be sure enough that the future indeed lies with them to dissociate themselves from those who continue in the old ways.

Yet some may still be anxious, contrasting perhaps the fragility of such a version of faith with the certainties of the past. Can the combination of critical scepticism and an endorsing of everyday experience properly speak of the God once proclaimed in creeds and by councils? Can such a God be 'true'? Academic discussion on this

in the last few years has drawn a sharp distinction
between 'realist' and 'non-realist' understandings of God,
and the view being suggested here would generally be
placed in the non-realist category. As a corrective to the
common assumption in everyday speech that 'real'
invariably refers to something that is concrete, physical
and totally objective, non-realist language is helpful. It
misleads, however, if it slips, as it easily can, and is
assumed to mean that God is *un*real or *un*true. For then
the term rapidly becomes a brickbat hurled at liberals to
indict them of atheism.

It needs to be said clearly that there is a great deal
within human experience that is no less real to us just
because we are not able to point to it or otherwise reify
it. Love, most obviously perhaps, is intangible and
wholly experiential, but still wholly real and true for us
in our lives. To say then that there is no objective
answer to the question of the truth of this use of 'God' is
to concede nothing that the honest traditionalist would
not also have to allow. However assured one's doctrinal
frameworks, whatever claims are made for 'historical'
events, there is no proof of faith. But experientially this
God is as real as anything else in life, as *the name we
choose to give* to these particular things that we
encounter as real. The use of the language of God itself
serves to invest these things with the significance we
sense they have, and develops that awareness further.
For it opens up dimensions of understanding that belong
with such language, but that we also find fit the
seriousness (serious in the sense of Philip Larkin's
description of a church building, 'a serious house on
serious earth'[12]) of these areas of our corporate and
individual experience.

Over and above that, and in terms of some of the more
classic formulations, such a view of God may actually
help to reclaim the language of God as creator, though
from a quite different angle to that which was uppermost
in the past before its basis was toppled by science. God

is apparent, we can say with conviction, wherever the creative power of love, compassion, truth, moral goodness and beauty is evident in human lives and in the world. And this is the authentic omnipotence of God. A quite different sort of power, to be sure, from that wielded by rulers and despots, and different from the old, imagined miraculous or magical ability to do anything in any situation. What it means, surely, is the capacity for God, understood in these terms, to be *made real* and realized in any situation where human beings have the will and the vision to want this to be so.

Further than that we cannot go. Fierce believers, no doubt, will dismiss open christians for that. Yet it is the view that religion must deal in absolutes that so much limits christianity today, and causes people to switch off from the churches. However much some may continue to be haunted by dreams of ultimate meaning, life is really too short to be hung up for long about such things. Whether or not these dimensions of depth and meaning do in any sense possess the status of being the ultimate purpose of life and of the universe we simply cannot know. But here and now they matter to us for sure. Simply and common-sensically they hold out a promise of life's worth to people when so much else threatens to destroy that. Since here and now is where we are all living, that surely is enough.

3

The worth of humanity

Retelling the story, redrawing the portrait of God in a way which, though less spectacular than some of the efforts of the past, can more truthfully mirror the life we all share, will do something to return the possibility of christian faith to the human arena. On its own, however, it is unlikely to achieve a great deal, since people are very aware of what they can only see as the church's disparagement of human skill, effort and striving; of how little time the faith has actually had for what goes on within the arena.

Traditionally, within judaism to some small extent but much more in christianity, humanity – actual men and women in their 'flesh and bloodness' – has not enjoyed a very good press. Lip-service may indeed have been paid to the idea of the 'glory of man', but a lot more effort and energy has been expended in telling of his misery and wretchedness. A phrase from one of the collects in the old Book of Common Prayer – 'we have no power of ourselves to help ourselves' – is in fact among the more gentle statements of the prevailing orthodoxy. Conservative christianity, treating the bible as the ultimate User's Manual for Life, has taken the myths about Adam and Eve and their offspring in the early chapters of Genesis to have the status of literal and (at least semi-) historical statements of how we got to be the way we are (instead of seeing them, as a liberal believer might, as early attempts to catch the dilemma of our existential apprehension of ourselves). So men and women are to be understood as fallen creatures, worthless and beyond any mercy, were it not for the undeserved and unearned generosity of God freely bestowed upon us. Between God and humanity a tremendous gulf is fixed. As Paul puts it in a classic phrase, 'All have sinned and fall short of the glory of God' (Romans 3.23).

This low view of humanity has sadly not been much moderated as new knowledge both of christian origins and of the human creature has become available. On the contrary, it remains central to the traditionalists' proclamation. On recent writer, Chris Wright, while obliged to allow the image of God in any human being, none the less quickly evacuates this of meaning as he replays this familiar theme: '. . . we cannot forget either that every human being is also a sinner and that humanity as a whole suppresses the knowledge of God available to them and that satanic deception has affected the race from the start'.[1] The result of this presupposition on the proclaimers themselves is clearly a tremendous absorption of time and energy spent persuading people that this is how they really are. Because the offer of this version of gospel is spiritual salvation, its recipients must first be told firmly how they are lost. Only if we have been convinced that as humans we are utterly depraved will we be able to appreciate what is, we are then informed, God's mercy!

Such a call to 'repent and be saved' is of course everyone's cartoon caricature of the evangelist. But it is clearly much more than mere parody. Just such a message, frequently in those very words, still figures prominently on the billboards outside many churches. It gets proclaimed in dire terms at all those evangelistic crusades by American preachers, which many christians who should know better are conned into giving support to. It is the image communicated by the pathetic gaggles of christians gathered at shopping centres at Christmas time or on Good Friday, apparently in order to make people feel guilty. And whatever might perhaps come of a Decade of Evangelism, it is the impression that it too

so easily conveys. That the church has got the facts that
the world would hear if only it could come to terms with
what, it is told, is the reality of its depravity.

This is not new, nor is its crassness peculiar to or only
apparent in the relating of christianity to the particular
setting of the western world in the late twentieth century.
If we look at the thrust of the European missionary
expansion that went hand in hand with western
imperialism in Africa and Asia down to at least the
1950s, we see that exactly the same processes, the same
clumsy efforts at selling a package, were at work. In that
context, though, surveying it from a distance, it is surely
even more apparent how ridiculous such an imposition
of a worldview on a quite different culture is. We see the
tragicomedy of the writing off of all that preceded
christianity's appearance on the scene as being quite
without worth. One wise priest, Hugh Maycock, who
served in Borneo in the 1930s, recognized it even then:

> A group of earnest missionaries entered one of the
> long wooden houses in a village and started enthu-
> siastically smashing to pieces the little images of
> pagan gods which they found there. 'The natives,'
> said Hugh, 'were too polite to object, too civilised to
> show their feelings and too religious not to be deeply
> grieved.'[2]

The arrogance of presuming that the church has
everything to give, and that outside of its gift all is
worthless or worse, is astonishing. Yet it carries on just
the same. Traditional christianity does not really allow
that there are other human understandings from which
it might learn, since all are bound to be the consequence
of sin and the Fall. It is true that Melvin Tinker writes,
in his own essay in the evangelical collection from which
we have quoted previously, of a need to attend to context
and culture when it comes to evangelization. 'If we are
to be faithful to the Great Commission to "make disciples

of all nations", then we have to be sensitive to the context in which the recipients of the gospel are to be found. To use the rather well-worn phrase, we have to start where people are.'[3] Yet the attention is quickly seen to be fairly superficial: '. . . when all has been done to remove archaic expressions, finding culturally equivalent terms, and so on, it remains vital that we help people think themselves into the Christian account of things. The concepts and terms rooted in Scripture are *fundamentally* [my italics] necessary for true *Christian* experience.'[4]

A further manifestation of this sort of dismissal of men and women outside of the church community at the present time is to be seen in the way traditionalist christians react to the arts, to writing and to the communications media. Thus a book by Andrew Walker entitled *Enemy Territory* is described by another evangelical author, Alister McGrath, as 'an excellent discussion of the strongly anti-Christian character of modern western culture'.[5] Can the role, the purpose, the splendour of the arts today really have been glimpsed at all if they can be summed up in those terms, one asks? And is such an assumption going to do anything at all to allow an exchange of understanding to take place between the church and that culture? Yet even this appears mild and restrained when compared with the views of David Holloway, the vicar of Jesmond, writing about radio and television. Christianity is gagged, Holloway claims, in its access to these media, for reasons that he then sums up:

> . . . it is not able to enjoy freely the responsible expression of views and values via the electronic media. Such limited expression as it is permitted is courtesy of an overall humanistic editorial and programming policy. Furthermore, 'religious' broadcasters in the establishment, good and Christian as

they may be, have no responsibility to the Christian
community itself, only to what seems to have become
a humanistic broadcasting hierarchy, with all the
pressures that can bring.[6]

A humanist conspiracy, then, is this traditionalist
believer's informed judgement on British radio and
television. It should hardly surprise us in a man
convinced that his christian faith was what stymied the
application for a television franchise in which he was
involved – 'If I had destroyed another man's family life
by seducing and running off with his wife, if as a
chairman of a big business I had ruthlessly destroyed
some small business, causing suffering, hardship and
unemployment, if I had advocated homosexual practice,
abortion on demand, and general sexual licence, I
probably would have been less handicapped than having
to say I was Vicar of Jesmond.'[7] You do not need to
doubt the truth of Holloway's professed wish in his
franchise application – which was simply to secure
better television for the north-east – to feel that this is
still wildly over the top. Certainly one understands how
people are likely to keep well away from a faith that
appears to dismiss so cheaply their human work and
achievements.

But christianity does not need to be like this when it
speaks of people. It has the resources to affirm human
life and its capacity for splendour, and open christians
must be seen to be doing this, and washing their hands
of what has been traded as christian understanding up
until now. The traditionalist view is unlovely and
repellent, and causes people to run a mile. It also
depends on bad biblical exegesis, as well as a distorted
account of our human situation. The biblical exegesis is
bad because the Genesis passages on which the whole
thing is built are not history, but myth. There never was
an Adam or an Eve or a Garden of Eden, nor is the
jewish author of these ancient stories ever likely to have

thought there was. The early chapters of Genesis seek to tell us, in myths, why things are the way they are: why snakes lack legs; why people speak different languages; and, in the myth of the Fall, why there is sin (or, more accurately, as we shall see in a moment, moral fragility[8]), and why life appears so laborious and painful, and ends only in death. The myth links these last two, and for its author it was the second part, clearly, that appeared the greater mystery. Why is this glorious life we have always cut short in this way? Why must we struggle to survive, and why does death appear in one sense to render all our struggles futile? Sin is the explanation that the myth, especially as it has been interpreted subsequently, offers for death. Before Adam and Eve sinned they would have been immortal. But having sinned, having disobeyed God, they are driven out of the garden where alone such immortality was possible. Thus this experiential fact of our mortality was provided with at least some sort of explanation.

There is a distorted understanding of humanity as well, however, that the traditionalists' insistence on having Genesis as their only resource makes unavoidable for them. No liberal believer, for all the charges that traditionalists sometimes like to press, would wish to minimize the frightening capacity in human beings for cruelty, destruction and hurt. In that sense evil is, of course, a very real possibility in all of us. It shows up in our actions as individuals and, even more, when it acquires anonymity in the corporate behaviour of groups – from street gangs to nations making war. It is more real indeed, and much more immediate, than much of the religious talk about 'depravity', and the allegedly literal account of a historically communicated taint, can very easily convey. Paul is faithfully recording a part of common human experience when he writes: 'I do not do the good I want, but the evil I do not want is what I do' (Romans 7.19). To some extent at least just such an ambiguity, a duality and ambivalence in the experience

of human life, is known to us all. We often do others
down, and we trample over them once they are down.
Both the present moment and our human history – not
least so much of the history of the churches – makes
this horridly plain.

Yet though all of this is true, it is still only part of the
picture. For human beings are also able to do good, to be
generous, to set aside self-absorption. We have capacities
for love, unselfconscious and unselfish, that are very
remarkable. We all witness this again and again in daily
life in any community. I think of instances I personally
have encountered in the course of my work: the love
seen in a woman as she tends and supports over many
months the husband who is dying of cancer; the love of
a parent alone – their going without things they need so
that a child can have a birthday or Christmas gift like
other children; the love of students giving time and more
so that physically and mentally handicapped youngsters
can taste something of the life they themselves enjoy.
The church's traditional story of our separation from
God – from God as the source of the good – really does
not do justice to the way we are, and the assertion of
total depravity does not square with the complex whole
of our make-up. Genesis is just too simple to be read as
any final word on this, as is the celestial rescue operation
performed through Jesus which is proclaimed as having
put things right. The fact is that good and evil are
present together in all of us; moral fragility is our true
situation. Alongside pointing to wrong and condemning
it, the proper purpose of christianity is surely to celebrate
the good and thereby encourage and advance it.

So recasting the christian view of human life means
starting here with the way things genuinely are, and
treating this with utmost seriousness. The church has
distanced itself from reality and people by holding out
no prospect for *this* life. It has gone on endlessly about
future glory, but in the meanwhile it has called upon its
followers to deny their experience in an orgy of

monstrously masochistic self-denigration. Christian worship makes this very plain, though regular members of congregations probably cannot see how odd and unreal it must all look to those who come to it for the first time. Church services, when they speak of goodness, ascribe it all to God, and when they refer to human beings they focus predominantly on their sin. You cannot take part in any main service in the Church of England without having to confess your sin, and Anglican clergy with their daily prayers can find themselves doing this three times a day. What possible reason could normal women and men have for wanting anything to do with a community that views life in this way? A mighty change is needed, for which the resources are all there, without slipping into any cheap or superficial optimism, if we can only look in a fresh way at the figure of Jesus. And that we need to do anyway, since traditional claims about Jesus bewilder those who are not churchgoers – and mystify many who are as well!

Christianity was formed and formulated, as we have already seen, at a time when the separation between God and humanity was understood to be total. Yet the heart of the conviction of the first generation of christian believers – something we see so clearly in the letters of St Paul – was that Jesus, through his life and death, had positively shifted how people felt about their standing before God, allowing and making it possible for them to believe that the great God/human divide might be overcome; indeed, *had* been overcome. If this were so though, according to the rules of the game that then applied, clearly he could not be *just* one of us. His roots must lie on the God side of the divide, even though he most certainly *appeared* as one of us. Here, in what at the time was the only possible explanation that would allow the experience they had known, we find the origins of the two great themes of subsequent christian theology: the doctrine of the Trinity seeking to understand God in such a way as to make room for Jesus (and the Holy

Spirit too), and the doctrine of the incarnation anxious to understand Jesus in terms of God.

Both doctrines actually took quite a long time forming. Only because we have them, do we tend to read the New Testament through spectacles tinted by them, and not surprisingly we discover them both there. We read them into New Testament passages, or we read passages capable of quite different emphases solely in those terms. (Just occasionally we get a shock. Christmas worshippers will be familiar with words from John 1.14 in something like the Authorized Version's 'the glory as of the only begotten of the Father'. The New Revised Standard Version translates the same Greek text rather differently: 'the glory as of a father's only son'. We discover words that make perfect sense, yet need carry no trinitarian overtones!) In fact it is unlikely that either doctrine would have been recognized, in developed form, by the first generation of christians. For what their attention really focused upon was first the continued aliveness of Jesus to them in spite of his death, and then that death itself as something needing to be explained. Convenient explanation lay to hand in the notion of sacrifice. For sacrifice was the traditional means by which humanity could approach God. The shedding of blood to please (appease) God allowed men and women to draw near. Now plainly the death of Jesus was in no normal sense of the word a sacrifice. It was a criminal execution of one who appeared to the jewish community and to the Roman occupying power as an unwelcome disturber of both the civil and the religious peace. But because the effects of the death (and of the life preceding it) were those that sacrifice had – the overcoming of the divide, the bringing close of God – then sacrifice was what it most naturally must be. And if it was, then what sort of a being must Jesus be if sacrificing him could have this effect? Clearly he must be made of something much more than the worthless stuff of fallen humanity which was the lot of the rest of us.

Jesus being uniquely a participator in the nature of the transcendent God makes perfect sense in terms of the presuppositions of the early christian period about both God and humanity. To say that it does not do so now for us is not to abandon faith, but simply to acknowledge that times have changed. The idea that God, even imaged in a quite traditional way, requires blood – regardless of according to precisely which interpretation of atonement the blood flows – is nowadays as much a moral affront to many believers as it is to people on the fringes or outside. We, even with all our fallibility, are more generous than that; how could less be expected of the one understood as Love? When we add to this the changed model of God-talk that was suggested in the previous chapter, it becomes very clear that we need a different approach, one that can do genuine justice to the humanity of Jesus in ways that the classic doctrines have not been able to manage. (This even more because, for many traditional christians, Jesus' humanity has almost always been something less than genuine. Did he really think as a man, or as God? Was he limited by the knowledge of his day? Did he appreciate his own divinity, and know himself to be the Messiah? Did he die knowing he would be bouncing back three days later? On many such questions, the answers of the orthodox rarely fit the orthodoxy they profess.)

If we take the language of God to be speaking about depths and dimensions within life, then Jesus is plainly not someone who leaps into play from outside the arena – which previously God would not sully himself to enter! – but someone who *from within* shows what a human life might be. Belief in the idea of a pre-existent divine person taking flesh just for a while in an assumed life has plainly had a very long innings within christian thought, and to many people must appear as a permanent fixture. Open believers who want to hand christian insights on for the future will see it differently.

As a notion it too is human-made and timebound, and holding to it is surely *not*, any longer, a prerequisite for being a christian believer today. Indeed, and outside of any desire to pass the christian story on, there are plainly already very many churchgoers who do not believe it, and there would no longer seem to be any grounds that could validly be advanced for censuring them or making them feel guilty. Only a superstitious supernaturalism such as indeed persists with conservative believers would provide any justification for that, and liberal christians will not wish to be saddled with it. It is past time that we took on board and worked through the consequences of words on this subject by Maurice Wiles, written more than twenty years ago:

> In the . . . cases of creation and fall our forefathers had to learn – and it was a painful process – that what they thought was a logically necessary link between the theological assertion and particular occurrences in history was not as logically necessary as they thought it to be. Are we perhaps at the equivalent – and even more painful – moment of learning the same truth about the doctrine of redemption?[9]

Accepting that that moment has come, it now makes much more sense (and there is never an excuse for *non*sense in religion any more than in any other sphere of life) to regard what has traditionally been called the divinity of Jesus as being quite simply the working out in his life, his teaching and also his dying of that spirit of God (God as meaning and purpose) which is there potentially, and deserving to be realized, in every human life. That places the emphasis back on our continuity with him, rather than on the discontinuity and difference that many traditionalists have tended to stress, with disastrous results for the accessibility of Jesus to ordinary men and women.

But I say 'places the emphasis *back*' very deliberately,

because the New Testament writers, for all that they stress the specialness of Jesus, did still see him very much as one of us. What had illuminated his life illuminated theirs as well, and while there was indeed a difference, given the framework with which they worked, it was much more one of degree than of kind. Jesus was 'the firstborn within a large family' (Romans 8.29). He was son of God, and so they too were the sons and daughters of God. He was the Christ, the anointed one, and they were anointed ones themselves. It is that perception that we need to take up again in order to reintroduce people to the portrait of Jesus. 'That which is of God in everyman' is a phrase that has long been cherished by Quakers, members of the Society of Friends, but it is wholly congruent with this powerful stream of New Testament understanding that we have to reclaim. So too is the Eastern Orthodox emphasis – generally neglected in the west – that sees the christian life as a process of deification. While in the past this has been understood as a gradual growing towards God, we can well reinterpret it to mean a progressive, developing, living out of the God within us.

In other words, incarnation, though it is not history, and though Jesus was a human being like the rest of us, is valid myth. That is to say, it is a story that illuminates the way life is, just as great poetry catches truths that prose description misses. The myth of God incarnate[10] was first expressed in terms of the life of the man Jesus, and it continues to cast light upon the existential experience of *all* women and men – thus showing us just what a human life can be. Geoffrey Lampe, surely one of the finest Anglican theologians of the post-war period, expressed this with great beauty and clarity – albeit with a kindly caution he was later less concerned to show – in an essay almost lost in the pages of the 1976 report of the Doctrine Commission of the Church of England, *Christian Believing*:

In the portrayal in the Gospels of [Jesus'] way of life, focused in his death as the key to the understanding of his life, there is to be found the supreme revelation of the relationship between God and man. Here is the great transforming and redemptive disclosure of God's judgement, compassion and love; so that the Jesus of the Gospels is God's 'Word' incarnated. Here is also the archetypal pattern of human response to God; it is a total possession by God's 'Spirit', or, in another image, an unbroken relationship of 'sonship' to God, expressed in freedom, openness, commitment, and dedication to the love of God, pursued to the point of death. To the Christian believer the Gospels mediate a supremely revelatory experience of God. He finds himself prepared to assert that 'the way things really are', or 'the way the world is made', is focused round this addressing of men by God in Jesus Christ and this compassionate love and the other 'fruits of the Spirit' disclosed in his life and teaching, and in the cross as the central point of disclosure. We Christians, as Professor Baelz has expressed it, 'see in Christ the ground for trusting and hoping in God, the example of trusting and hoping in God, and the source of inspiration and power to trust and hope in God'.[11]

Jesus provides the type for humanity, setting the style for a particular way of living. His purpose for us, his worth to us, is to show the possibilities that are there within us.

People who are onlookers upon the christian community will be quick to point to the problems that remain in this, and particularly in stating it too naively. *The* type for humanity, I have said. But since there is no longer any literal historical 'incarnation' to appeal to, that clearly is a statement made only out of faith conviction. The 'bestness' of Jesus is not something that we have any way of proving. It may make sense to the members of the community of faith, but it cannot be demonstrated for certain to those outside. *A* type for humanity is as far as we can honestly go. But what kind of 'gospel' is that? If we want to commend christianity to others, how can this sort of understatement possibly suffice? The point is one frequently made by conservative christians, anxious to stress the necessity of standing by the uniqueness of Christ. Chris Wright damns the kind of view of Jesus I have been advancing in terms of 'supermarket mentality', 'relativism' and even 'coffee table books'.[12] The loss of exclusivity, both for Jesus and for the christian religion, is seen as implying the loss of everything: '. . . if Jesus was not more than a man,' writes Wright, 'then the whole Christian faith and all the generations of Christian worship have been one monstrous, deluded idolatry.'[13]

But outside of the camp of the biblical fundamentalists – and Wright's use of the New Testament is wholly literalist, and allows no room for modern criticism – I doubt whether such arguments truly count for much. Indeed, it is probably the case that it is this sort of exclusivism, the invariable link of conservative proclamation with the need to do other creeds and philosophies down, which is a big part of what so repels people from organized religion today. Does the worth of my creed have to involve the dismissing of others? If standing in the tradition of Jesus has genuinely illuminated life and living for us, what makes it so necessary to say that he must do so better than anyone else? Are conservative convictions perhaps less confident than is always claimed? It is at least possible – flying a kite for a moment! – that some of the church's saints were gentler, more compassionate, more self-forgetting even, than Jesus may have been. But if it was still *his* example, and life in the community that looked to him, that made these saints so, then what of it? For this is all part of the continuing incarnation which is the heart of our human worth.

There is the further substantial problem, implied in

part in this, of how much we actually know about the
life and character of Jesus. Increasingly, New Testament
scholarship makes us aware of the creative role to be
ascribed to the gospel writers. We cannot straightforwardly assume that the picture they paint for us
provides historical truth. And if they do tell it true, there
are other problems no less real. How are we to cope with
the fact that for many of his contemporaries it was
obviously Jesus the miracle worker, Jesus the magician,
Jesus the exorcist, who drew the crowds, not Jesus the
proclaimer of the kingdom of God? And more difficult
still, how do we respond to the unattractive elements in
the portrait? There is Jesus the fanatic, Jesus the
extremist, and Jesus the one who could apparently
dismiss and disregard the love and concern of his family,
who needs to be faced as well.

It is right to be aware of these things, for if we are
hoping to share a renewed christianity with others this
is a part of the story we must tell, and not something to
be hidden under the carpet. There has been too much of
that with 'orthodoxy'! But the problems are in a sense
no greater than those we meet when we consider any
figure from another age. It is only the Christ of dogma
that requires to be protected from the realities of
belonging to a particular place and time. Jesus the
firstborn of many brothers and sisters, Jesus who
proclaimed a gospel of the kingdom of God (rather than
the object of a gospel the church later, however quickly,
fashioned round him), does not need to be sheltered in
this way. We may accept that he was in many respects
different from us – and in some ways different also
from the gospel portraits of him – and yet still find our
inspiration in a tradition begun in people's experience of
him and now renewed in us. It is clear that many people
do respond to the figure of Jesus and find it fascinating,
despite (or maybe because of) his being rooted in his
time, and certainly in spite of many things that they
simply cannot believe about him. Well beyond the

confines of the churches he draws many who care not at
all about incarnation or resurrection. Open christianity
wants to work with this realistic interest in the man, but
does not seek to turn it into the kind of dedicated
idolatry that 'orthodoxy' so easily becomes. For if what
Jesus himself proclaimed was indeed that God is known
in the here and now – 'The kingdom of God has come
near', the first words ascribed to Jesus in Mark's gospel
– then it is probably truer to his purposes that we
should not always be looking back to him.

Jesus offers – borrowing some words from John
Bowden used towards the close of his masterly *Jesus:
The Unanswered Questions* – 'a clue to how the world
is, to how we are, to how God is, even if at times the clue
seems cryptic beyond our understanding'.[14] As such he
points us not back to final tidy answers, not even in
himself, but forward to new questions, new challenges,
new possibilities for giving reality to that worth of
humankind that he showed in a life lived. If that seems
too low-key to old-style believers, if it offends by the
standards of what religion has sometimes claimed to
offer, it is likely none the less to be a great relief and
encouragement to many others. Overstatement in
religion is actually what destroys its credibility for
honest people, what undermines its claim to speak in
any way of truth. Acknowledging this, recognizing that
the role of Jesus is something more modest, may well
allow the authenticity of a recast christianity, and so
breathe fresh life into him as its inspiration.

4

Faith in life

Our last chapter said nothing about the resurrection of Jesus, and not much about the significance and importance of his death. For some this will have seemed strange. If we were wanting to show Jesus as the one who permits us to speak of the worth of humanity, is not the resurrection both the evidence we need for giving our attention to him and also the clinching proof of that worth? Men and women are not like the beasts that perish, without understanding. In the resurrection of Jesus, for those who are faithful, there is the promise for his followers of life beyond physical death.

It is certainly the case that christian traditionalists have often spoken in these terms. The resurrection, it is claimed, does away with any need for the sort of hesitancy that so typifies liberal believers, and marks Jesus out as much more than simply an example. One stalwart of English evangelical fundamentalism, Sir Norman Anderson, identifies resurrection in one of his many books as being right at the heart of faith, one of the three central tenets of orthodox christianity (along with incarnation and the cross as God's unique remedy for human sin). He puts it thus: 'that he was in fact raised again on the third day, and that this resurrection must . . . be regarded as a divine authentication both of the reality of his claims and the efficacy of his atoning death'.[1] Anderson here is pushing an extreme view of the resurrection as the *proof* of Jesus, but in his defence, at least at first reading, he may not appear to be that far removed from St Paul:

if Christ has not been raised, then our proclamation has been in vain and your faith has been in vain. . . . If Christ has not been raised, your faith is futile and you are still in your sins. . . . If for this life only we have hoped in Christ, we are of all people most to be pitied. . . . If the dead are not raised, 'Let us eat and drink, for tomorrow we die' (verses from 1 Corinthians 15).

Yet statements such as this, clear as they may seem to be about the centrality of resurrection talk to christianity, are actually far less clear when it comes to identifying what this resurrection is and what it means. When, moreover, writers like Anderson attempt to rectify this, to make them clear and turn them much more precisely into proof, then it is obvious that, while this carries conviction for some, it positively antagonizes a large number of others. The notion that talk of resurrection is what gives christianity its power, what allows it to offer comfort – for instance, in the pastoral context to people who have been bereaved – is nothing like as straightforward as its proponents want to maintain. For the moment you start unpacking resurrection into factual statement and event many christians – let alone those who are not churchgoers – back away in incredulity and disbelief. Clergy unsympathetic to open christianity will be quick to tell you how David Jenkins's Easter sermons at Durham when he became the bishop there enraged and distressed believers. Honesty requires me to say that I know from experience with my own congregation that this is clearly so for some people. Equally clearly, however, such non-literalist approaches produce great sighs of relief in others. As with the virgin birth, the physical resurrection is something that many faithful christians can only sit light to.

The difficulty lies, as we have seen before, in some people's desire to have things cut and dried, and the feeling that nothing less is appropriate to religion. The amount of effort traditionalists have put into 'proving the proof', the countless volumes of the 'Who moved the stone?' variety, the excitement generated by the Turin Shroud, and the further string of books that appeared when it was being seen as possibly the historical evidence for the resurrection, all witness to this. (They may also, perhaps, suggest that subconsciously among the faithful all is not quite as sure as is claimed!) St Paul, it is quite clear from his writings, did believe resurrection was something of great importance to the faith that sprang from Jesus. But he would have been much more cautious – it seems every bit as apparent – about spelling it out too closely, trying to define it as some once-for-all event. His own faith – as witnessed in the same chapter of 1 Corinthians that was quoted from above – seems to have been based on some kind of experiential appearance of Christ as risen, an experience he says was shared by at least 500 others of the first generation of believers. But of the empty tomb, so important to the gospel writers who followed him some years later, Paul shows no apparent knowledge. Certainly he did not think it necessary to report it, or claim it as 'evidence'. Moreover, his version of 'appearances' differs from the evangelists', just as they differ among themselves. And the earliest gospel, Mark – if we accept the view of the growing number of New Testament scholars who consider 16.8 to have been its intended ending – while it holds out the promise that Jesus will be 'seen' in Galilee, provides no accounts of this at all.

In that sense then, we may say that there is an allusive character to resurrection stories and, indeed, to resurrection faith all the way through the New Testament. And the reason for this is that it really is not – for most of the writers – the easy 'happy ending' or the reassuring proof that it has so often been turned into since. Nowhere in its pages is resurrection seen, as so often since – in a damning but accurate phrase of Donald MacKinnon's – as 'a descent from the cross postponed for thirty-six hours for dramatic effect'.[2] For indeed, as he again points out, it is the *un*believing world that cries out 'come down from the cross that we may believe in you'. The New Testament writers are trying all of the time to hold the death and new life of Jesus firmly together, and to maintain the connection between them and the life that preceded them. The thing is a whole, and either it rings true as a whole or else no amount of 'proof' will convince anyone about any of it. In St Mark's austere account of the crucifixion, the divine sonship of Jesus – whatever we mean by that – is already apparent to the centurion who stands close and looks hard at that from the way in which Jesus died. He requires no resurrection tacked on afterwards to convince him. By contrast, for the women who stood a long way off at Calvary and so did not see, and in spite of their being depicted as members of the close band of Jesus' followers, resurrection adds precisely nothing to the nothing they had grasped thus far. When they come to anoint a corpse in the tomb and are told that no tomb contains Jesus, they flee terrified and speechless.

All of which, I believe, offers encouragement to us in attempting, with integrity and truthfulness to the nature of the world as we experience it, radically to restate resurrection faith today. Such a restatement will not be trying to smooth out or remove the elements of faith and hope that are genuinely central to it, nor will it be wanting to make resurrection easy, straightforward or logical where before it was mysterious and haunting. What it will seek to do is focus the faith, the hope and the mystery where they really need to be placed. Which is not on an extraordinary event, but on an experience that offers a remarkable window, as it were, on to *ordinary* life, the life that as human beings we all of us share. For behind the stories (the appearances, the empty tomb, and the later additions of earthquakes, angels, the dead rising and walking, the flabbergasted guards, the grave clothes neatly folded and the rest), and carried by these but not bound to them as if they were history, what the first christians are struggling to express, what they are seeking words and images for, is their faith conviction that in the case of Jesus at least evil has not enjoyed the final word. Nothing literally undoes the death of Jesus, for nothing can. What resurrection is trying to say is that this death has not undone his life. The cross is not the curtain pulled down, the end of a lovely drama but one now seen simply as fantasy. This way of living is understood to remain valid and true, death notwithstanding.

So the key witness to christianity's resurrection faith lies in a sense, as some of the catholic Modernist writers recognized at the beginning of this century, in the persistence (indeed the coming into being) of the church after the death of Jesus.[3] Where it might have been expected that that death would be played down, or the evidence of it suppressed, it actually becomes the heart of the proclamation. It does so, in terms of our discussion in the last chapter, because it is seen, however oddly, actually to vindicate the life that he lived. The meaning and purpose that were seen in Jesus throughout his ministry acquire their full significance in his willingness to stick with them to the point of death. And that in turn encourages the disciples to keep to the way of Jesus, in the faith that somehow he continues to journey with them. This is really something felt rather than stated. When the earliest followers do want stories to explain this, they tell them with the glorious freedom of people bursting with trust and hope rather than proof – 'This is life, it feels like hope', making full use of ideas such as resurrection and the gift of the spirit, and often (in John's gospel at least) untroubled by a considerable blurring between the two.

Jesus' resurrection, we are saying, is to be most helpfully understood not as the promise of some sort of physical life beyond death either for Jesus or for those who look to him, but initially as the sense that his followers had of the vindication of the example of Jesus in that one life which, in common with all the rest of us, was his. To quote David Jenkins in one of his Easter sermons, it is about the 'cumulative, personal and faith-filled discovery by the first Christian women and men that Jesus, his life, his continuity, his hopes and his challenges had not been cancelled by his crucifixion'.[4] Seen in this way, all the problems and improbabilities that have to do with tombs and appearances fade into comparative insignificance, for this is not about such things, and does not depend on them, even though they may serve to paint a picture of it. It was with such an understanding that Geoffrey Lampe was able to draw a firm distinction between christian believing and any need to subscribe to a literal raising of Jesus from death when he wrote:

> The continuity between Jesus then and 'Christ' now does not seem to be dependent on a personal, still less a bodily, resurrection. If the bones of Jesus lie in Palestine – and where else may they be? – this is no hindrance at all to our encounter with, and response to, the saving and quickening presence of God the Spirit who perfectly possessed the spirit of Jesus and is now re-making us after his likeness. If the present state of that human person of Jesus is beyond our speculations, this is part of the general mystery of all the departed.[5]

Words like Lampe's, and probably the whole approach of this chapter, will no doubt appear shocking to many in the ranks of conservative believers. But within the purposes of this book, and for the sake of open faith, a clear and unqualified statement of what can be said by men and women true to the perceptions and under-standings of their day seems vital, and can only be for the good. First, and this is not insignificant, because it may do something to help lift that burden of guilt, that quite unnecessary fear of being caught in unbelief, which

I suspect is felt by a good many christian people, laity and clergy alike, who have found their own way to such an understanding. There are plenty of them, we know. When the 'Durham Affair' was in full swing in 1984, the Church Society (a very definite conservative evangelical group) commissioned a poll on the beliefs of church-goers, probably with the hope that it would show how out of step David Jenkins was. What it in fact revealed plainly was just how many christians did not believe the historical status of either virgin birth or resurrection. More recently, the work of the Rural Church Project has further indicated that almost 31 per cent of churchgoing Anglicans (from a survey of 489) do not believe in life after death.[6] So there are already a lot of open believers about. But Easter triumphalism often unnerves them, causing anxiety about their right to the title of christian. It really should not. Such an understanding is reputable not only intellectually – there can be no doubt about that – but also spiritually, for it is well rooted in christian origins and closer, in its spirit, to the convictions of the first generation of believers than much of the superstition that passes for resurrection faith among the 'orthodox'. Christians who hold such views have no need to be tormented by self-doubt.

Nor, and this would be the second benefit of honesty on the matter of resurrection, should they keep quiet about where they are and maintain a discreet silence. For such an understanding, if it were spoken of plainly and without embarrassment or apology, could well serve to give fresh credibility to resurrection talk outside of the church community. For because it has been limited in its reference almost entirely to what Lampe called 'the general mystery of all the departed' (though insisting, of course, that there was no element of mystery or hesitancy about it!), the traditional use of resurrection language has appeared pretty nebulous, sweet-sounding 'pie in the sky'. Not only this, but so far as most thoughtful people are concerned, it has had the effect of damning the whole of the church's faith as wish fulfilment divorced from any reality. So for anyone still anxious to present christianity as a credible creed in the modern world (as well as for those they have tried to address) it has served not as 'clinching proof', but as a major obstacle. Once freed, however, from its reference to Jesus' alleged personal survival beyond death, and from its limiting to something similar for the rest of us, resurrection has a chance of beginning to be seen as having some bearing upon our own lives in the here and now. It is worth quoting David Jenkins again, in his 1988 Easter sermon:

> The happening of an extremely mysterious and unlikely event, even if it is of a man coming alive again after an undoubted death, is just that – the establishing of an extremely mysterious and unlikely event. The question for faith or for hope or for wonder or for praise is still 'so what?' What is going on here? What is this part of? How does this reach out into the whole of human life and the whole of the world we live in?[7]

Well, how does it? What in practice can this mean, removed from the world of make-believe? For the first disciples, it was suggested above, it was as if the meaning and purpose they had seen in Jesus actually acquired a deeper significance through his holding to them to the point of death. This in turn encouraged them to keep to that way, for all the varied hurt that was part of it, in the conviction that he journeyed with them. What they saw as at work in Jesus and now in them was the stubborn refusal of love to bow down to unlove. This in spite of all the force and apparent success that attaches to the latter.

The parallels to such experience are there in many settings today, and in the lives both of individuals and communities. Sometimes, with some, this will arise from a conscious desire to imitate Jesus, but at many other times it happens quite independently of any such prompting, when the same human spirit surfaces in people who may well be wholly without knowledge of the church's story of Jesus. Recognition is all that is needed – though even lack of recognition cannot diminish the reality! Wherever light is able to shine through in life, whenever goodness and practical kindness win against uncaring or cruelty, resurrection is at work. So there is resurrection in the person offering an afternoon's respite to her neighbour in his task of caring for a demanding, elderly parent. There is resurrection in the community that can welcome the halfway house for those discharged from the local psychiatric hospital. There is resurrection in governments acting to bring an oppressive regime to change its ways (as well as anti-resurrection, we would have to admit, in bankers' previously helping to maintain it).

Viewed in these terms, resurrection is something profound, yet utterly ordinary as well. Far from being a religious oddity, something 'all over the mountains, where the beautiful go to die' (words from W. H. Auden's 'Shepherd's Carol'), it is really *just life*; life showing itself able to count for more than the unlife that is so apparent in the workings of the world. Resurrection is the faith that the good person is not to be beaten by the apparent meanness and mean-mindedness of the world. In terms of current servitude to 'the market', it vindicates the refusal to be conformed to the mentality of 'grab what you can get', pointing to one who achieved such refusal and who lives on in the community that looks to him. What it does not do, contrary to the claims of so many religious conservatives, is provide any sort of magic answer to life's intractable mysteries and in-justices. Resurrection cannot pretend to solve what is called 'the problem of evil' in any of its many forms. Too much deceit has been uttered on that, and followers of a new christianity need to come clean. What it does do is offer a different perspective on it. John Robinson, who in the 1960s with his book *Honest to God* helped many more hesitant christians to maintain contact with the church community at that time, articulated this point very clearly in a sermon printed in a final posthumous collection, talking specifically there about the inexplicable randomness of physical and mental illness:

> The problem of evil is not how God can will or allow it . . . , but its sinister power to threaten meaninglessness and separation, to sever and to sour, so that, in Sydney Carter's words, we lash out against 'the million angels watching and they never move a wing' and are blinded from seeing God *in* 'the carpenter a-hanging on the tree'.
>
> For the Christian no more than for anyone else is there purpose or intention in the ravages of a cancer. . . . It is not the cancer or the paralysis, the haemorrhage or the schizophrenia, that represents God's will for persons, but precisely the transcendence of these blind, sub-personal processes, whether by cure or acceptance, in the power and freedom of a truly human life.[8]

If all this is rightly to be understood as resurrection, if this is the 'faith in life' that the christian story encourages us in, what more is there still needing to be said about death with which, in the past, resurrection language has been so closely linked? Much of the power of traditional christian faith and imagery for previous generations was certainly linked with its ability to address the fear of death. But that fear would seem to be nowhere near as great for us as for our ancestors, not least because a full and long life is now likely for so many more, though it would plainly be naive to imagine that it will disappear simply through the force of rational argument. A fear of dying is likely to be much more real an anxiety for many, perhaps as a consequence of death being that much less familiar to us, and even here new use of medication to relieve pain without dulling of consciousness is doing a great deal to allay this. Dying well, the reordering (and, indeed, renewing) of life before death, is itself nowadays an instance of the sort of resurrection experience I have been advocating for many more than in the past. Overtly 'religious' death-bed scenes may not feature much today, and that is probably no great loss. But at a deeper and more natural level, dying and death certainly allow – as I am very aware as a priest permitted to share in such moments – for reconciliation and healing of hurt to take place in many instances, with much good issuing from them.

Yet still a sense of the *waste* of death remains strong for many people. Is all this glory to become nothing? Stepping out from our own situation can make this yet more urgent. For, from the very different perspective of those who lack the western comforts that allow us to think of life as good, is there to be no redressing of the injustices of this life? Perhaps I have tasted enough of eternity to be satisfied; what, though, of the starving child in Ethiopia or the Sudan, or the young students mown down by government troops in Peking, or the civilian victims of the Gulf War, or whoever are next to suffer hurt of this kind? For many people, only the assurance that such things will be righted beyond death will allow them to speak of God, whatever that name may point to. Without that, all religion appears blasphemy.

The argument is cogent, and not to be dismissed trivially, but at the end of the day it still appears mistaken. For it is bound up with that old model of an inactive yet omnipotent deity which for all kinds of other reasons we have now seen has to be abandoned. What such questioning about the waste of life really points to is the vital requirement for all people of goodwill to be seeing the need for, and working at the means of, a more practical resurrection here in this life, worked out in these settings and all the others like them. That does indeed leave things untidy, in terms of the unanswered questions. But really there can be no answers, and it would be best if we simply admitted that this is so. To quote Geoffrey Lampe again: 'It is perhaps rather comforting that what Professor Hick calls "eschatological verification" can only work one way: it can only be positive. Either the hope of life beyond death will turn out to be true or we shall not be there to find it proved false.'[9]

Yet to leave things even at that point may seem to many now, with more than a decade passed since Lampe's death, to be itself too much of a fudge. Life beyond death has, during that time, come to seem increasingly unlikely – not least because, in the way in which christianity has preached it, it is built upon a separation of humanity from the rest of the animal creation which it is surely going to become impossible in the future to sustain. If then we are not going to be there beyond death – albeit that we shall never know this – does that rule out the use of the language of resurrection and eternity in the non-ultimate way in which I have employed it? Have I myself now moved into Alice's Wonderland, a realm in which language in fact means nothing since it is alleged to mean whatever one wants it to? Can we only honestly speak in this way, as the traditionalists would indeed want to claim, if it is a foretaste of something more?

I think not and, for the sake of those liberal believers and half-believers for whom all the old talk of life beyond death is a major obstacle to their feeling part of the christian community, it seems important to say so clearly. Extinction is not the absolute we often treat it as. It does indeed seem almost certain that there will come a time when I am not, in terms of the self-awareness which makes me 'me'. This self will wholly cease to be. But neither I, nor anyone else, has ever existed in isolation. Life of necessity touches other lives, affects other lives, and for good or ill (which are matters over which we do have a great deal of control) in some sense changes them. The processes of reproduction, the passing on of genetic coding, ensure this for the great majority of women and men. But not simply that. Those who have not in fact produced offspring to carry their genes will also live on, however obscurely, in others, who will themselves in turn live on in one or both of these ways. If then humanity carries what we speak of as divinity within itself – which is the heart of the recreation of christianity which we are concerned with here – we are all in this way kept within the 'mind of God', of which our human minds and hearts are the physical expressions. For the christian, Jesus is once again the exemplar of precisely this. A traditionalist's statement of faith may wish to say that he lives in God in the heavenly realms. What we know for sure is that he lives in his church, in and through the lives of countless millions of believers.

If we can only allow ourselves to accept it, this is actually a far more dynamic and creative mode of resurrection than any that was promised to us beyond death by an older view of faith. For it allows genuine room for growth, and change and development in the 'me' that is handed on, beyond whatever point I shall have reached personally by the time I die. Jesus has himself been regularly recast by his followers down the ages. Sometimes, to be sure, with fairly disastrous results as we read the accounts of the church's history! But frequently creatively, his insights adjusted to different settings, new cultures, and knowledge and worldviews of which he could never have dreamed. When the author of Hebrews wrote of Jesus being 'the same yesterday and today and forever' he spoke nonsense, as the whole story of the church makes plain. Jesus' resurrection has come to mean not the immortalization of a first-century rabbi, preserved in aspic to be reverenced for all time, but the living growth and enlargement of the ideas and the lifestyle he communicated through human beings unable to allow these to be lost. If this resurrection of his is to be regarded as in that sense the fruit of his vindication in God, so too is mine. That is not in any way the reductionism it is so often dismissed as by the traders in heavenly promises. It is as much as we need, or can expect, to be able to say. It gives life a value and significance that allows us to have faith in it.

5

Renewing the world

What is it in practical terms, in application, that is going to follow from the change in christian perspective that we have been exploring until now? We see resurrection as a way of speaking about the significance of life here and now, life *before* death indeed, and we take eternal life to be a reference to the handing on of what we represent, what we have done and what matters to us, in lives that we have touched, rather than any sort of personal immortality in eternity. This certainly does lead to a shift in the focus of what christian living is held to be about. The old emphasis on heaven almost inevitably made faith seem very narrowly personal. *My* salvation, *my* survival was at the crunch what mattered and what it was all felt to be about. So alongside the undervaluing of this world, the poor relation of that to come, there was also a distorted perception of it. The interrelatedness of human beings was always something of secondary importance when compared with the unique, individual self which was charting its solitary journey towards God. That was what counted and what must not be allowed to be compromised.

Aspects of this sort of understanding are clearly not wholly worthless or without value. Our experience of totalitarianism in the twentieth century reinforces all the knowledge that we have of it from previous periods in making painfully clear what can happen when the individual is lost sight of through deferring to 'the general good'. Yet however dreadful that may be, it must not blind us to the fact that other dangers flow from forgetting that human beings do not exist in isolation, or prevent us from recognizing that there is an inevitable social dimension to our life alongside of and with one another. Frequently much traditional christianity has missed these things, and still does. The logic of a recast christianity must be that the world and human society both matter. The kind of approach to them that was for ever marking them down in comparison with eternity cannot apply now that that eternity has gone.

Many traditionalist christians would indeed be anxious to claim that they are concerned for this present life as well as for life beyond. In the last few years a considerable amount has been written from these quarters about particular social issues, and a number of lobbying groups now exist which would not have been dreamt of even quite recently. Yet a closer look at so much of what has been said, and at the activities based upon it, makes plain how difficult it is for uncritical and supernaturalist christians genuinely to escape the constraints of the understanding they have taken upon themselves. Landing on my desk within a few weeks of one another at a time when an election seemed on the cards in Britain during 1991, were two invitations to question local parliamentary candidates – one from a christian group and the other from the World Development Movement. The latter, as one might expect, was a meeting about issues to do with Britain's relationship with developing countries – 'aid, debt, trade, arms sales, the global environment' were the things listed, clearly expressing that Movement's concerns. But they are issues, it is plain, that would ring bells for many others as well, despite their being outside of its formal membership.

The christian group's leaflet was no less clear as to what it saw the real election issues to be. Billed as an evening to discover whether parliamentary candidates *care*, it invited questions on 'such issues as abortion, pornography, Sunday trading, broadcasting statements'. There is a feeling almost of entering another world.

Without wanting to claim that any of these subjects are
necessarily trivial or peripheral, the perspective is
certainly a very different one when we encounter them
linked together in this way. We have stepped over from
themes that have universal significance, care for the
planet and for life within it, to what cannot help but
appear to be the essentially private concerns of a
somewhat self-absorbed sect. The last item on the
shopping list – 'broadcasting statements' – makes this
particularly plain, since what it thinly veils is a desire to
discover whether the politicians will allow commercial
radio and television to be used for conservative christian
proclamation. The centrality of this for the protagonists
of 'orthodoxy' is explained by David Holloway, whose
priorities are very plain. Having discussed at some length
the failure to his mind of 'permissive' broadcasting, and
urged a 'christian' correction of its ways, he explains
why. 'It is vital that the *essentials* of the Christian faith
are heard in the Public Square. We do not need a
Pelagian gospel. True, we must talk about social justice
and personal morality, but only *after* we have talked
about the love of God in Jesus Christ'.[1]

Readers of such views and material outside the
churches very quickly draw their own conclusions as to
what believers apparently think matters and, sadly, what
that indicates about christianity. For myself, finding out
a few weeks after receiving the public meeting leaflets
that at a diocesan event in my own area someone was
speaking from an allegedly christian perspective about
the *dangers* of the Green Movement made it painfully
obvious to me just how blinkered and sectarian we have
become. For the dangers being talked about were not
threats that there might be to the future of the planet
which the Movement had overlooked, but its alleged
irregularities according to the dogma of christian
orthodoxy!

To say that is to identify the heart of the traditionalists'
inability to respond in any adequate sense to the issues

of life today, and the point from which open christians must chart a fresh course. When we talk of living a christian life, and such a life as is able to take seriously the world and human society, we are entering the area of ethics. And historically it is the case that, within most religious traditions, ethical behaviour has generally been taken to mean life lived according to a particular set of rules. Such rules can vary in their precision. Within the Old Testament background to christianity the best known to most people will be the Ten Commandments, which are themselves quite broad injunctions. Other material within the jewish writings however, and indeed the more typical, is much more focused and precise. The law books of Leviticus and Deuteronomy especially provide very detailed instructions as to how life is to be led by the Israelites both at the individual and collective level. Some of these instructions are still quite frequently trotted out by christian commentators as determinative for our actions and behaviour today. The recourse they have to them is, however, highly selective. Passages that accord with a wish to condemn homosexual expression or to maintain the subordinate status of women are proclaimed fiercely to be permanently binding. But other instructions of parallel status in the original codes – from the prohibition of charging interest on loans to the many rules about dealing with ritual impurity arising from skin diseases, itches and boils – are quite happily overlooked!

If we ask why those instructions that are treated as binding should be regarded as such, we will be pointed to their alleged divine validation. These are laws that God has given, in line with the claimed general divine authorship of scripture which was looked at in Chapter 2. However, no informed understanding of the bible or of the nature of religious writings can properly support that view. The legal codes that have come down to us from judaism are not peculiar to that community, but are in most respects very similar to many others that were around at the same time in the ancient Near East. Israel's laws clearly reflect views that were current across a wide area at that period about the ordering of society, quite as much as they do that nation's own particular faith. They are, we must say plainly, a wholly human work: a systematized and finely tuned attempt to articulate both common sense and the consequences of belief in God in the form of a series of laws about behaviour within the life of the nation. The claim that God has been personally involved in them obviously helped stress their authority, and maybe even did something to assist their observance, but it can have no status for us today with our knowledge of the origins of such texts.

When people fail to recognize or admit the human handiwork that is the reality of allegedly religious 'law', as conservative christians are bound by their systems to do, they absolutize a particular point and moment in human understanding with disastrous consequences for those who follow. For they absolutize also the very specific patterns of social and economic life that pertained to that period, and the whole package of 'values' that supported these, and try to bind people to them for ever. Pragmatic traditionalists may find ways of circumventing some of the more barbaric ordinances of the Old Testament books – the stoning to death of adulterers, for instance – but they are still trapped when it comes to passages of teaching ascribed to Jesus in the gospels which have been regarded as definitive and law-giving. At least, they are trapped when it comes to the area of individual, 'private' morality, so closely identified with the achievement of individual salvation. Take one very familiar instance. The church community continues to trip itself up over what Jesus may or may not have said on the subject of divorce because, whatever that was, it is alleged to be permanently binding. (This, despite the fact that an honest, critical approach to the gospel texts would quickly make plain that from very early on christian leaders were having to adapt and adjust the hardline views that Mark's gospel claims that Jesus held.) The same anxiety over holding to what are alleged to be the authoritative pronouncements of this pre-existent divine being is however not seen to anything like the same extent when the subject under consideration is wealth – in spite of the clarity of Jesus' teaching on this! Nor do we see much desire at present to uphold his view on the ties of family, for which he seems to have had very little time.

The difficulties, however, go further and are much greater than this. Deferring to the worldview of the past not only binds you to particular pieces of teaching when their appropriateness has passed, but it also prescribes for ever those areas of life and existence that can be the subject of ethical reflection and moral judgement. Either that, or else it causes us to try and derive moral principles from rules laid down for quite different areas to the ones that actually concern us now. The inevitable result of this is that the realities of the present situation get discounted. In that checklist of alleged 'christian concerns' already referred to, none – even if you were to accept that these are the real moral issues of our day – could be described as immediate concerns of any of the biblical writers. So conservative christians must manufacture support for their absolutist opposition to abortion, for instance, from traditions generated in the second-century world and from general biblical positions on the sanctity of innocent life, without giving attention to the hard questions about this matter that press upon us now, and on which the bible – even if it were authoritative – is silent. What constitutes life? Is 'existence' always the highest value, even when it involves misery for the one brought into being, or the parent, or indeed both? If the rules can be held – as they generally are! – not to be absolute when it comes to taking life in war, is the embryo in the womb and incapable of independent existence really, and on every occasion, in a quite different category? Such are some of the real and very hard questions that the issue of abortion presses upon us, and they are not to be resolved by any amalgam of biblical platitudes and emotional blackmail.

Or consider again those 'broadcasting statements', which would have been even more beyond the comprehension and concerns of either Old or New Testament writers. The impetus behind conservative believers' desire to have access to the media for proclamation lies in what is sometimes called the 'Great Commission', Jesus' apparent instruction to his followers – which is found at the end of Matthew's gospel – to 'make disciples of all nations'. But whatever the import of that – and New Testament criticism would certainly have questions to ask about the ease with which those words can in any sense be honestly ascribed to Jesus – today's world has other considerations that cannot simply be set aside. What about the power of broadcasting in contemporary culture and the abuses of indoctrination to which it can fall foul? Conservative christians are quick enough to complain about this when it comes to what they allege to be a liberal humanist consensus. Should not their anxieties about that carry over into their own use of the media? Or what about the context of a pluralist society within a small nation, where so many creeds and understandings coexist? Does not that suggest, indeed require of those whose views are not wholly bound by their personal religious assumptions, that some moderating of the 'Great Commission' may be necessary to safeguard social harmony and avoid ideological discord? Are there not distinctions needing to be drawn between information, education and evangelization which have to be applied to the public media? In a democracy, party political broadcasts must be controlled rather than bought, be labelled as such, and be made available to all major parties. Does not religious recruiting (which to the impartial observer is what evangelism amounts to), without discussion or right of reply, need to be no less controlled – regardless of whatever the bible or any other religious textbook of a particular group may or may not happen to say?

Timeless moral absolutes do indeed have a certain superficial attractiveness in a world of change, but always at the expense of treating seriously and sincerely the genuine complexity of life. One easy solution according to the rulebook lets down and fails a whole series of other people and circumstances which are not to be lightly dismissed by the language of 'exceptions'. When therefore open christians renounce the claim that anything has been given for ever, their honesty is likely to be welcomed and appreciated by many other people who are aware of the need for hesitancy in all talk of 'truth'. We must say straightforwardly that there just are no *rules*, in that old-fashioned sense of dictates from outside that are binding upon us.

What christians do have, not as rules but as example, are the reported responses of Jesus (some his own and others, surely, his followers', attaching their ideas to him) to particular moral situations in the light of his own response to God. We must be honest in admitting that *his* background, *his* circumstances and knowledge all limited him in his dealing with these things in just the same way that ours limit us. So even when we address ourselves today to areas of human experience that he addressed, it does not follow that we shall think the same thoughts or reach the same conclusions that he did. When it comes to other areas – and most are such – where the stories about him provide no guide, the link will be slighter still. But that is not to say that it is non-existent. It lies in the broad and deep principles with which Jesus himself and his followers can be seen to have been working, and which if we see them as still having some worth and importance we will be trying to apply in fresh ways in order to take up today's needs.

Principle rather than law then. Of itself that is hardly a dangerously new approach. Within the New Testament gospels we could call it, though it over-simplifies, the way of John rather than of Matthew. Matthew makes use regularly of the old rules that are already there. His Jesus therefore has the Old Testament laws still binding upon all believers, and in every detail. 'Do not think that I have come to abolish the law or the prophets; I have come not to abolish but to fulfil. For truly I tell you, until heaven and earth pass away, not one letter, not one stroke of a letter will pass from the law until all is accomplished' (Matthew 5.17, 18). John opts for principles or, to be more accurate, for one principle, that of 'love'. It is this undoubtedly that makes John so superficially attractive to many christians today, and explains the regular resorting to the gospel for readings from every occasion from weddings to funerals. In fact, of course, the application of the principle in John is very limited. Though Jesus comes for the world, salvation is *from* its ways and understandings. Love then is something pretty restricted, applicable only to the community of the already redeemed. But given that, 'love one another' is all that needs to be said. Working it out can be left to believers provided they are loyal to the community to which they belong.

Right through christian history – even if believers have not always been ready to own up to it – the church has been obliged to make use of principles in this sort of way, in the absence of any specific teaching, across a whole range of areas. The umbrella of 'love' contains many strands that can be observed in the story of Jesus (and which are not so narrowly church-based as John might have wished) which can be drawn out and developed. These include: self-sacrifice, forgiveness, generosity, gentleness, humility; the principle, in the light of the gospel, that the alleged 'eternal order' of how things are may be not only challenged but reversed (the hungry fed, the lowly lifted up); a view of life understood as gift and so to be responded to with thankfulness. All these and more have come to be seen as being available for the christian believer, to be unpacked in the particular circumstances of the life both of individual and of society. Guided by them, it has in fact proved possible for the church regularly to reassess its view of the world and to say some quite new things. During much of the last century many believers could still consider such practices as slavery, or the subjugation of women to men in a whole variety of ways, or child labour and the removal of children from their parents, or the public execution of criminals, as all being consonant with a christian understanding of life. Save maybe on the matter of women's rights, few would do so now. The rules of life have shifted through a fresh application of the principles. Sometimes christians have helped initiate the process of change, while at other times the lead has come from elsewhere, but the result has been the same. Shifts in understanding of what is 'right' and what is not take place within both the church and the wider society, and both, whether together or singly, alter the church's perception of the gospel it has received. 'Time,' as the hymn says, 'makes ancient good uncouth'.

Something of this process operating and also faltering can be seen if we look briefly at that area of prejudice which in so many ways still remains to be righted – that of the subjugation of women. Here, though in the wider society there may be much that is far from ideal, it is noticeable that the church continues to lag behind. The ordained ministry is closed to women in both the Roman Catholic and Eastern Orthodox churches, and in much of the Anglican Communion. In the Church of England, at the time of writing, women can only be ordained as deacons, the third of the historic orders of ministry and so, being denied ordination as priests, cannot preside at the celebration of the eucharist, the holy communion service. Even if current legislation to change this passes, which remains uncertain, women will still not be eligible to become bishops.

There is now a considerable literature on this issue,

written both to defend the way things are and from the
other side seeking to change them.[2] To the open believer
in sympathy with the approach of this book it will be
quite obvious that the reasons for this exclusion are all
bound up with the absolutizing of the past. Judaism, in
the biblical period, was a patriarchal religion, just as
Israel was a patriarchal society. In the context of the
ancient Near East it would have been hard – though not
impossible – to see things otherwise. So nation and faith
together built upon the Genesis creation myth a view of
woman as always subordinate to the male. Women were
part of a man's property; sometimes, to be sure, they
could be referred to with tenderness, but on other
occasions they were lumped in with the rest of his
possessions, along with the cattle and the household
goods. It was the male who ruled over the household as
he did over the nation, and who in most settings
therefore naturally served as the cultic religious function-
ary as well.

Christianity took over these views and arrangements
from its jewish parent and did not see any reason to
depart from them. It may be the case, as some christian
feminist writers have been anxious to assert, that Jesus
was more open to women than others in his day and
welcomed them into the inner circle of his friends and
followers, but the gospels' witness to this is not really all
that clear. It is perhaps wiser to avoid special pleading
and accept the fact that 'there is no positive evidence
that Jesus saw anything wrong with the sexism of his
day'.[3] Certainly when it came to the apostles from whom,
by various routes and in any number of different ways,
all subsequent patterns of christian ministry have been
held to derive, these were all male (though it is not clear
that in the first century the distinction between
'apostolos' and calling Phoebe in Romans 16 'diakonos'
was clear in the way it has become to many since then!).
And again this is quite understandable. For anything
else to have been the case would have required some

sort of christian cultural revolution, and these things just do not happen with religious matters in isolation. St Paul was able to say that 'there is no longer Jew or Greek, there is no longer slave or free, there is no longer male and female; for all of you are one in Christ Jesus' (Galatians 3.28). But in practice, racial separation, slavery and male supremacy all persisted in christian societies. Until members of society as a whole see something awry in this, religion moves with the rest of the pack.

Nowadays, however, in the understanding of male and female throughout the western world, that revolution has occurred. Steadily, across the whole field of human activity, the division of task and responsibility on the basis of gender has been eroded. Women now occupy senior positions across a wide spectrum of jobs and careers (albeit after a struggle and with quite a bit still to be achieved), while men share in domestic duties previously regarded firmly as 'women's work'. The 'head of the household', where that term has not been consigned to the historical dustbin, can be female or male in today's society, as can the head of the nation – monarch, president or prime minister. And so the only real choice for the church is a very simple one. Does it accept that its ways in the past have been culturally conditioned like everyone else's, and so fall in line with the rest of society, or does it try to claim some sort of distinctiveness for its past? Claim, that is, that it was separate from the rest of what was going on, however much historical and sociological understandings may appear to make plain that it was wholly a part of it.

Realistically, I would suggest, there is eventually only one possible outcome to all this, given the experience of christian history in other areas of life and the changes already under way in many branches of Anglicanism and in most other christian churches also. And it would surely be best to be honest about this. The kind of attempts that have been made to reconstruct the christian past – like that of trying to show (as was referred to above) that Jesus was much more radical on this than had ever been realized, or else to prove that later generations of christians did not really regard the ordained ministry as a male preserve – are probably dishonest and, for a recast christianity, quite certainly mistaken. For they serve to perpetuate the myth that the past (which bit of it, though?) is somehow normative, that it contains all the answers that we have need of; however, it is this misunderstanding that we so desperately need to escape from.[4] Tangles such as that over women's ordination, or divorce, or the physical expression of love between people of the same sex, will persist and get worse – far worse as the rate of change and development increases – until we escape from the illusion of believing that the last word on everything (anything!) has been said.

To state this, in the light of christian history, is not really to be laying claim to anything new. But to treat it positively, to celebrate as a virtue of faith its capacity to change its mind and to think fresh thoughts, rather than be having to hide these things away as embarrassing departures from the rules, that is a quite new step. And a step that, if christians can only take it boldly and without prevarication, could contribute a great deal to the renewing of the world.

First, because it would rescue *us* from the curse of dealing in minutiae. The issue of the equal status of women and men for instance, which is what underlies the whole discussion of women's ordination, is certainly not trivial, but it is one that most people outside the christian community have long settled already. It mystifies them that believers have not, and offends and distresses them as well; there really are more important things to be moving on to. So long as our story binds us to imagined inflexible truths from the past we cannot do that, for moving forward on anything takes an age when it is necessary to appear to be always deferring to the past. Accepting that we work with a limited number of insights and principles drawn from our perception of the God of Jesus, along with the best information available to us today, we could for our present time resolve the issue of the dignity and status of the sexes (and those of divorce, and homosexuality, and others besides) very speedily. Then we could get on to some of those wider themes that already exercise and involve so many of our fellow human beings, and that an open christianity ought certainly to be able and wanting to address. These would include issues of the discrepancies between the western world and what we call 'the Third World'; issues of the environment – its perils to the fundamentalists notwithstanding; issues of the weakening of society and the undermining of the sense of our responsibility for one another in this and so many other western countries. Some of these issues will be considered further in the next chapter.

Second, and surely no less important, because our own freeing from the myth of laws which are claimed to bind us for all time could then do something to help rescue many *others* from the elusive quest for the definitive answer, the perfect solution. The illusion that truth must be absolute if it is to be in any sense worth while is certainly a powerful one. Within the church it is surely ironical that we can even see it being perpetuated at present by a cause so valid in itself as that of women's ordination. In much that is written there remains the illusion that, once this is sorted out, all will be well and the church will achieve the status of that perfect society which, under God, is its due. But of course that is not so! Ordaining women to all the orders of the church is a big step forward for our time, but those who follow us will see plenty of other continuing imperfections, unknowable to us, in whatever we pass on to them. More generally, outside the confines of the christian community, we find this same platonist myth persisting in the strong feeling across so many fields of human activity: that by trying just a little harder we could get everything right; for instance, some within the field of medical research at the present time believe that we shall soon have access to all the mysteries of life.

The legacy is strong but ultimately very debilitating, and it leads easily to despair. If the church, which has been so responsible for its influence upon western thought, were to let it go, this could mean a real freeing for others too. The answers to life's mysteries and challenges are not just around the corner, though it is a perennial delusion to think that this must be so. We solve one set of problems only to discover others. Our worldview moves on so that we see some things more clearly, but at the same moment we begin to catch sight of how much still eludes us as further horizons are opened up. There is nothing to suggest that this experience is other than infinite. What does seem likely however is that human beings will actually be able to achieve more, and achieve greater contentment in the process, through coming to accept that we can only do the best we can, with the knowledge at present available, for now. Our yearning to see things whole must not be allowed to prevent us from seeing them as they are for the time being. Openness means owning up to the fact that recasting and renewal is ceaseless, as a prelude then to getting on with it for the present moment. Strangely, we shall actually do the job much better once we have accepted that our successors will before long be needing to do it all over again.

6

Valuing what is ordinary

Religions have traditionally claimed to deal in more than just ordinary things. Christianity's central myth speaks of the divine, the supernatural and transcendent, literally coming down into the natural world, and as a result of this action and its consequences being able to take humanity up into that heavenly paradise for which we had been intended but from which we had fallen. There are good reasons, we have seen, why that myth can no longer convince on any such literal terms, and why it requires decent burial if christianity is to begin to be recast in a form that speaks to people again. However, the change, even when it is recognized as necessary, is not without difficulties. The old stories had indeed become nonsense for most people, but they were an impressive sort of nonsense none the less. The very fact that there are liberal believers within the most conservative of religious institutions is in a strange way a testimony to the power of these myths. Though we could not believe them, they still drew us – and served to inspire the sort of restatement that is the concern of this book. But once that work is done, is it possible that such a renewed christianity, however attuned it is to how we think and feel today, can itself attract people? Or does it become too pedestrian and prosaic to merit attention, almost as if irrationality were somehow central to religion and an essential part of its appeal?

The point is one that is often made, even if it is not expressed in quite these terms! Maurice Wiles, while himself maintaining the validity of the liberal approach, puts it clearly and well in words he wrote in 1973:

It is sometimes argued that Christian belief is impaled inescapably on the horns of a dilemma. It can either be stated in a strong form, in which it is interesting but almost sure to be false. Or it can be stated in a weak form, in which it has some chance of being true but ceases to be interesting. A robust incarnational faith which speaks of a God who has lived a human life and died a human death; that would be a faith which had bite to it, a faith worth believing – if one could. But hedge and qualify that understanding of incarnation and the faith will die, if not of the thousand qualifications themselves, then of the boredom of its own attenuated claims.[1]

With a few caveats from some, perhaps, about too easy a use of the language of 'truth', that is a summary that would carry conviction for many in both the pro- and the anti-religion camps. Whatever our recast christianity, they would say, it is not religion in the full-blooded sense that they would feel those who want such things expect. Our open and non-dogmatic emphasis on life in this world is something that seems to belong rather more to the setting of humanitarian good works and social care than to the religious arena. For if religion does not deal in other worlds, it surely ceases to be religion and is better dispensed with.

This is a view that certainly appears convincing, but only for as long as one is taken in by the veiled over-simplification so characteristic of much religious argument. It is true, of course, that conservative religion ('proper' religion, its adherents would want to say) makes great play with the notion of other worlds. Yet despite this, when it actually comes to the crunch, even the most flamboyant recourse to such language and imagery only makes sense if it is used, as it regularly is, in relation to *this* world. The transcendent god who remained aloof in transcendence would be utterly unknown and unrecognized by us. The god must communicate, the other worlds must somehow interact with this one, if they are to be at all significant for us. The jewish and christian faiths have been particularly strong on this, with a god who speaks, who sends messengers, and eventually in Jesus arrives in person. And that is just the classy end of the interaction. In popular religion there has been a multiplicity of other levels of engagement, with all those good angels and demonic spirits as the creatures who were capable of crossing regularly between worlds, interweaving the supernatural into the natural, either creating havoc or else helping to sort it out.

Rational women and men may well smile at this, seeing it all as just another quaint survival of nonsense. Yet the fact that this is certainly what it is does not alter the terrible harm that such ideas are once again able to cause through the practices they give rise to within conservative christianity. This would be bad enough on the lunatic fringes. In fact, the last twenty years has witnessed a revival of a whole range of bizarre activities, including such things as 'faith healing' and 'exorcism', within many quite mainstream churches. Supernaturalism certainly seems to be on the advance as conservative religion's last rather desperate attempt to command the public stage. The results are doubly tragic. It works its own disasters in the lives of many people carried along by it (people who are frequently psychologically disturbed and emotionally vulnerable), and at the same time serves further to alienate most average people from the possibility of giving religious expression to their lives.

I regularly meet people who have dropped out of the church's life, or who are now embarrassed and discouraged survivors on the fringes of it, because 'healing services', 'prophecies', or 'speaking in tongues' have been imposed upon the previous patterns of worship (which they were able to cope with) by enthusiastic supernaturalists. These latter, with their naive patter about 'God's Spirit' being at work, are the ones who then complain so much, of course, about the growth of the occult in contemporary society when they see children putting on witches' masks for fun at Hallowe'en. Their own responsibility for a much more serious revival in occult nonsense, their dealing in demonology and what they claim is 'deliverance' – this, not surprisingly, they refuse to acknowledge. Just occasionally, however, it will slip out unawares, as in these words of Canon Tom Walker's: 'Many clergy found to their personal cost that there were many people both inside and outside their congregations who had dabbled with occult practices, and also they were called on to pray for psychologically damaged people who were frequently to some degree in bondage to Satan.'[2]

When possession by Satan can be talked of as a cause of psychological illness, and exorcism be advanced as a way of dealing with such conditions, conservative clergy and their congregations (their victims, I want to say) really are playing at a medieval version of christian faith again, but without any of the justifications of being people of the Middle Ages.

There is a grotesqueness about the way conservative christianity now employs such practices to maintain its myths of the supernatural. For that is clearly what it is all actually about. Another evangelical writer, Gervais Angel, indeed says as much, in an otherwise fairly cautious examination of the appeal to miracle in today's church: 'The ecstatic, bizarre and supranatural miracles are to be judged not for their character as ecstatic, extraordinary, etc, but for their effect, that is, whether they promote faith, hope and love like any other form of miracle.'[3] The apparent acceptance of the whole thing as in that sense some kind of publicity exercise or boost to recruitment is as alarming as whatever is claimed to go on. There is no reason to doubt that people can indeed be affected by such beliefs and rituals. We have learnt the power of ideological brainwashing during the twentieth century in politics as well as in religion, and the evidence is all around us.

But the cost is very frightening. For religion, when it operates in these ways, boldly discounts reason and takes positive pride in setting it aside. Supernaturalism is indeed obliged to do this, for the dismissal of the natural in its highest forms – human intellect, human skill, human understanding – is required in order for it to take root. To justify asking people to take this sort of step, the claims for the miraculous have to be forever hyped up, while the significance of the world's normal workings is discounted. So never mind, for instance, the continual work of healing and making well being done through the careful skill and loving attention of doctors and nurses. Whatever lip service may be paid to the worth of this, the real McCoy, the mark of God at work, is healing by magic in the churches. Even that, though, may come to seem rather tame after a while, so that we find it becomes necessary in several settings to throw in a little raising of the dead as well! So far has the Church of England gone down the line of gobbledygook that (I have been told by students working with me) in at least one theological college where future clergy are trained it has been stated by one member of staff that failure to believe that God works in these ways only proves the students' lack of faith.

If the issue of asserting the transcendent in today's church is, when it comes to the crunch, increasingly often about this sort of allegedly supernatural meddling in the world, open christianity need not be apologetic about having no truck with it. The claim will be made, of course, that good does come out of some of these practices, that people are made well and healed. But in general, when it comes to such 'cures', it would seem the case that natural processes, or normal but perhaps unacknowledged medical procedures, are what are actually at work, and deserve to be recognized. That is certainly the view of those who have studied the evidence from outside the circle of 'practitioners' with their personal interests. While in other areas, where the talk is of 'deliverance', the real need is to expose the fraudulence of systems which, by first encouraging people to think themselves enchained, actually contrive to enchain them – systems that then compound their dishonesty in quite shamelessly going on to proffer a way out of the captivity they have imposed. It is a sad truth that the demons from which people can be conned into believing that they suffer, and from which unscrupulous religion claims to release them, are all of them religion's own products. The ministers of conservative christianity, like the witch-doctors of other cultures, create the very fears from which they then offer release. Control is sadly what it is all in the end about.

Religion does not have to be like this, however, and a faith that does not rely on binding people with such debilitating transcendence is what a recast christianity needs to offer. The challenge, indeed, is to take up the ordinary and the everyday not as poor relation but as a thing of worth, and draw out from it all the richness that is there. It is a matter of very great urgency that this should be done. For at the other end of the spectrum from the religious occult, secular materialism has traded on a debased view of human beings as nothing more than consumers, requiring a constant supply of fresh products in order to secure some temporary satisfaction. So the world in its turn becomes essentially just a package of resources, there to be plundered at will. In this way, and however ironical or perverse it seems, materialism has actually played along with the traditionalist christian emphasis on human unworthiness and its writing off of fallen humanity.

Yet there is that other whole dimension to how human beings are which we have touched upon earlier, and which this misses completely and fails to take seriously. This is something well brought out by A. N. Wilson in his splendid polemic, *Against Religion*, which here as at so many points deserves to be taken very seriously indeed:

> One of the strange and rather attractive features of modern life is how highly kindness and generosity are valued. Of course it can be sickening when pop stars or other public luminaries make displays of their charitable endeavours, but it remains true that charity and unselfishness are very widely valued for their own sake. Different generations invent or reinvent their own cardinal sins. In this generation now aged sixteen to twenty-five, I should say . . . that the cardinal sins were racism and cruelty to animals. One can laugh at the earnestness which this sometimes produces, but on the whole it makes life pleasanter rather than the reverse. . . . The impulses to 'feed the world', cherish its wildlife, to make life more bearable for ethnic and other 'minorities' are manifest and palpable among enormous numbers of young people today.[4]

Wilson is wanting, quite naturally, to make the point that this human generosity and reverence owes nothing to religion. And in terms of the old supernatural versions, the perils of which he denounces with all the accuracy of one who knows them from the inside, this is surely right. What a refashioned christianity must take up is a much more positive 'naturalism' which is at the heart of what Wilson perceives. 'In empirical terms, it is simply untrue that when religion is discarded, the human race starts to behave very badly or to think cruel and unkind thoughts.'[5] Just so. It is the innate capacity for goodness in women and men, this ability that is to be found in so many spheres and instances for people to look beyond

themselves and their own needs, that a new christianity
ought to be celebrating and nourishing. There is in fact
no need for the supernatural – over and above there
being no possibility of it! – once we have grasped this
capacity for the natural to delight and surprise. The
ordinary is actually so much more extraordinary than
old-fashioned religion has ever been prepared to allow.

For the old view, locked as it was into its pre-
conceptions about human depravity and original sin,
could never allow any human goodness unless on the
basis of the grace of God. This was never our own, but
always something implanted in us from outside as a
supernatural corrective for the failings of our natural
state. Only 'Holy Spirit', the distribution of which or of
whom was a church-mediated exercise very firmly 'under
God', could enable us to overcome our natures – and
even then not all that often. But such deceit will no
longer do. Once we set supernaturalism aside, 'Holy
Spirit' ceases to be a foreign body to the human system
and becomes rather a dimension to every human life,
both individually and in our human interrelatedness as
well. It is quite simply the name that we give to the sum
total of human creativity, generosity and goodness.

This is not – we need to say quickly – a wishy-washy
cosmic optimism which disregards all the things that
fail to fit in. As has been stressed earlier, there clearly
are many other sides to human nature, and many forces
at work in us that are far from attractive; a good number
of these religion has been quick to make use of and has
frequently exploited. Nevertheless, what we may call in
religious terms the 'original righteousness' in people has
gone on surfacing and shows itself to be no less powerful
than the 'original sin' that so much exercises traditional
believers. And in every setting. Free acts of kindness
and generosity, as we have suggested already, are things
to be found in any local community. Neighbours look in
on someone who is ill, and will offer themselves to cook
meals or to fetch a prescription. An elderly churchgoing

woman with her husband in hospital finds that the couple next door, with whom she only ever exchanged a few words and whose children's noisiness in the street on a Sunday morning she was often wanting to criticize, are quick to volunteer the transport to the hospital that she needs. A couple who have just moved into their new home discover a note pushed through the door asking if anything is needed to help settle in, and with it a list of useful local information. All these are normal, human actions, and yet ones that say something about the power of love. They may be done by christians, but they may equally well be the actions of people with no specific religious commitment. They certainly have nothing to do with supernaturalism. They are wholly ordinary, and yet utterly and delightfully surprising: the extraordinary dimension of the ordinary, which both supports and also reinforces our profession of faith in life.

A christianity that recognizes this and welcomes it without mean-minded caveats – the new christianity for which we are arguing – will approach the rest of life and the world to which it is glad to belong in terms not of conflict and controversy, indicting others and determined to put them right, but with warmth instead. And all the time it will be looking for, and expecting to find, friends and allies instead of foes. Meeting with people of other traditions of faith, it will approach them wanting to discover common ground rather than anxious to point up their error. For past generations this has been virtually impossible, as other faiths have almost invariably been viewed by the standards of a christianity understood as somehow absolute. Open believers, however, must escape this particular strangle-hold, building upon their recognition that theology is always made by men and women, not handed to us from outside. We may understand how our christian forebears saw their faith as absolute because it was so for them; because its worldview supplied the parameters for every aspect of their lives. But we need not now follow them in that exclusivism. For other people, other traditions of faith have functioned in a similar way to our own, and achieved a similar authority.

Hence we are not required to shed our conviction that christianity still possesses much that is of worth, in order to start approaching others without necessarily assuming that they must be inferior; that they are there to be converted to our ways; and that there is nothing we can learn from them. We may still feel the need to test their traditions against what we have learned from (and brought to) christianity. We may even at the end of the day still want to say with humility that they are lacking in some ways that we are not. But the criteria for this will need, as John Hick has observed, to be empirical rather than arbitrarily given. So we will need to ask of each tradition such questions as 'Does it produce greater holiness?' or 'Has it led to finer societies?' than other faiths. Honest answers will certainly not be reached easily, and for every point any tradition may score it will probably forfeit others.[6] And if at the end we still wish to say that it makes sense to be a christian in Europe because of the opportunity to share faith convictions and to apply them with so many others, that ought not to prevent us from wanting to co-operate with people of other traditions on many shared tasks. And it should allow us positively to acknowledge and affirm that they have a similarly full value for cultures other than our own.

Nor should this open outreach be limited simply to other *religious* faiths. Having itself moved beyond some of the old, narrow formularies of 'religion', a renewed christianity will equally be seeking friends in those many secular creeds that recognize human worth and wish to improve men and women's circumstances. Liberal humanism and western European socialism, for instance, are both in a sense offshoots from the main judaeo-christian tradition. The liberal believer will recognize that there were good reasons that prompted their parting company in the past, but will want now to re-establish contact and cultivate shared understanding. While supernaturalism must be reckoned dead as a framework for living, the task of drawing out the dimension of the extraordinary ordinary which is written into life ('transcendent immanence' in the old religious language), and so freeing women and men from the tyrannies of poverty and hunger in the Third World and those of undervaluing and dehumanizing in the west, remains something vital for all people of goodwill. There is indeed a need to exorcise the demons that continue to oppress too many people, but the resources for this lie not in any heavenly magic but within ourselves, part of that glory of humanity which we are wanting to celebrate and extend.

If that is our task in common with our fellow humans, it is surely also our responsibility towards the natural world. If traditional christianity and secular materialism have combined to diminish people and their worth, they have both had similar – and of late much more devastating – effects upon the planet we inhabit. Harvest festivals notwithstanding, christianity has generally discounted any idea of there being a sacredness that belongs to nature. Those who defer to biblical texts as authoritative over both our thoughts and actions have homed in on the command in the Genesis creation stories to 'fill the earth and subdue it; and have dominion . . .' (Genesis 1.28). They have preferred to ignore those other passages in the bible that speak of the earth's need, in common with that of women and men, for a sabbath's rest (see Leviticus 25). Historically, therefore, the church's view of nature has been only slightly less crudely that of a resource to be plundered than, say, that of Stalinist communism in Russia between the 1930s and 1950s, or most of the western world with regard to oil resources until the present day. Though there have been some other more positive strands in the western tradition, most notably perhaps the eighteenth century's discovery of 'nature', it is surely telling that the latter was part of the Enlightenment reaction against religion, not a christian repentance for past neglect.

People in all settings are seeing things differently now, however, and christian people must learn to do the same, regardless of whatever the bible may or may not have to say on the subject. Our freeing of christian faith needs to value nature as nature: that is to say, extraordinary and wonderful in itself, and not requiring to be made 'respectable' through any ecclesiastical blessing. Christians need the honesty to recognize that this is one area certainly where their own tradition has been gravely lacking, and be open to illumination from others. Where the religious traditionalists see orthodoxy outraged by the New Age movement and the like, liberal believers would do well to approach it a little more openly. Though there is a good deal about the New Age which is as naive as old-fashioned christianity, with a surreal, spiritualized 'nature' taking the place of the traditional spiritualized heaven, there are more rational strands within it to which it would be sensible to attend. The American monk Thomas Berry has written from within an open, though cautious, Roman Catholic perspective of the urgent need to reintegrate the human story into the earth story. Berry criticizes the New Age approach precisely because it is too mystical and spiritual, because 'its proponents don't understand that the story of the universe is simultaneously a physical-material story as well as a spiritual one'.[7] But he criticizes the general approach of western capitalism still more, and by implication that of the church as well, for losing sight of the interweaving of the human community with the rest of the natural order:

> Human economics is crazy; to have a rising gross national product with a declining gross earth product is obvious disaster. The first law of economics must

be to preserve the integrity of the gross earth product. . . . The urgent question now is whether the industrialised human is a viable species on earth.[8]

A rational, non-emotive 'greening' of open christianity is part and parcel of our valuing what is ordinary. Letting go of the old escape route of supernaturalism, which is what made it possible for christians to dismiss the world in the terms of John's gospel from which we started in Chapter 1, requires this of us. Where traditional christianity separated human beings off from the rest of the natural world as being alone 'in the image of God', we have to weave ourselves afresh into the whole of which we are part. We created that distanced God which then allowed us to distance ourselves from the rest of life, and to distance religion and spirituality from the rest of ourselves. That lie is past. The everyday, life lived in the material world, albeit a world full of surprises, is all there is. We can dismiss it on those grounds and so despair, or we can marvel at it and rejoice at working with it to bring about the good, but we cannot escape from it to anywhere else. Patrick White provided as one of the epigraphs for his remarkable novel *The Solid Mandala* words from Paul Eluard: 'There is another world, but it is in this one.'[9] His story is at one and the same time utterly ordinary in the lives it recounts, and yet, for those characters in it whose eyes are open, quite extraordinary as well. Those who live fully are those who are alert, to borrow the book's closing words, to the 'actual sphere of life'. A new christianity must be encouraging us all in that same realism.

7

An open church

What place is there going to be for the church in a christianity reformed along the lines that we have been suggesting? We have certainly used the word in the previous chapters, and talked there about a possibility of a new style for the christian community. Yet in reality the whole thrust of what we have been arguing for is challenged by so much that the church has represented in the past, and by what it still plainly means to many of its members. Against our emphasis on looking for common ground with other people and welcoming allies, the christian church has most frequently defined itself *against* other faiths, and often other versions of christianity also – let alone 'secular' patterns of under-standing! No other religious tradition, with the single exception of islam, the other 'People of the Book', has been so sure not only that it is right and true, but that it has a monopoly of truth and rightness which must constantly be promoted to those who are in error. *Extra ecclesiam nulla salus* is the classic phrase that has been taken to sum everything up – 'outside of the church there is no salvation'. The ferocity of the struggle between christianity and islam in the Middle Ages is witness to the strength of this conviction then. The fact that it is being re-enacted today in ways little less violent from both sides in various parts of the world is evidence of how, for many people, things have not really changed at all.

Might it not be better then for open believers simply to let the institutional church go? Some would argue so, and not least on the grounds that any association, even

one dedicated to openness, in practice cannot help but
define itself in contrast to others. Hence barriers arise
almost spontaneously, however much we may want to
deplore them. As A. N. Wilson observes: 'It is a well
attested human phenomenon that a group of wise men
and women, when formed into a committee, start to
form foolish resolutions. Swell the committee to a crowd,
and it becomes capable of madness.'[1] Others would say
that the kind of association that the church represents is
simply unnecessary to the worldview that we are
advocating. This pattern of christianity is surely a life to
be lived, rather than a philosophy or creed that requires
institutionalization or self-conscious celebratory gather-
ings. Any such processes are going to stifle the openness
so central to what we are about.

There is force in these arguments which deserves to
be treated seriously. There is also, it needs to be
acknowledged, a very real possibility that the increased
hardening of conservative christianity will mean in any
case that those who respond to such a renewed version
of faith will not find themselves accepted within the
institutional church as it stands, even if they should
wish to be there. Already such exclusions effectively
happen within traditionalist congregations. For many
conservatives, credal statements and dogmatic tests
seem to have become proportionately more important,
even as others revolt against them. If such hardening
continues and gains ground, any alternative church
structure that open believers felt moved or required to
create would plainly want to be a very different sort of
community from so much of what is around today:
humbler, less absorbed in itself and its customs, and
committed above all to genuine attention to that whole
world of which it is happy and grateful to be a part.

Yet with all these caveats, there would seem to be at
least three good reasons for the continuance of some
modified kind of church, some sort of christian
association, for those who are open believers. If the time

were to come when such people were excluded by the mainstream churches, the first need would surely be a network that allowed them to make contact with one another. This could probably be met by something quite minimal – at its most simple, indeed, perhaps little more that a directory of names, addresses and telephone numbers. This is a model that does already exist in embryo in Britain, though only to a very limited degree, under the aegis of SCM Trust. Yet though the provision might be basic, people united by a particular perception, and with a common approach to life and the things of life, would surely want there to be this means of sharing their concerns together. Liberal christians will indeed be embarrassed by the emphases of the church's past, and by its perennial obsession (apparent again in Decades of Evangelism and Evangelization) to persuade or cajole others into joining it. Still, this is not an inevitable consequence of things shared, and a reformed type of christian association, freed from just this sort of obsessive concern for recruitment, could well begin to take on new significance for many people.

In particular, some sort of church could have a part to play for open believers precisely because they are not people who are buttressed against life's ambiguities by the mock assurances of creeds and dogmas. For the very fact of their openness, their honesty indeed, means that they are not able to close their eyes to all those dimensions and ingredients to life which conflict with what they have named as God, and all that flows out from that. Seeing these things, and unable either to pretend that they are not there or to take refuge in an omnipotence which one day will put them all right, many may at times come close to despairing. The wooden assurances of conservative believers, their apparent blindness to such things, serves only to make matters worse.

Hence the place for a reformed and open church as the setting, or at least the structure and framework, within which people can celebrate with others what they most desire and believe to be true. There are dangers, clearly, in allowing that to run wild. It certainly does not mean giving free rein to escapism, nor taking on all the attributes of a group of ostriches together. It is more a matter of assisting one another to see things whole, and recalling to one another the vision glimpsed as being something that is also valid and real, alongside of whatever else would seem to indicate otherwise. This is not something that mainstream christianity has been at all good at, and particularly not during the rapid changes of the last 150 years. In a world whose ambiguities have been increasingly apparent to many, the church has preferred to pretend that things are other than they seem. The excessive assurance of so much that it has tried to say has effectively cut it off from any who dare to acknowledge the greys of existence rather than pretending that all is a matter of black and white. So many of the gospel stories of Jesus depict him operating on the edges of society, dealing with people who were marginalized from the mainstream, and thus hesitant. The church as it has existed of late seems both unable and also unwilling to relate with people of this sort. An open church, one that saw its role as being at heart more a matter of giving support rather than of increasing its membership, could strangely very well discover that it was actually somewhere to which others would want to draw close. Honest people, unable to swallow the requirement to believe six impossible things before breakfast, yet attracted by a body that cautiously, and without naive pretence, can speak about life's meaning and worth.

So secondly, at least for some, it seems realistic to think that the framework of a reformed church community would expand to become something more than simply a communications network or directory. Ideally this would want to be built upon the churches as they exist today; only if they could not accept as a part of themselves this kind of open christianity would it become necessary to envisage a completely fresh start. For some version of the activity of worship would still appear to be capable of touching and inspiring very many people, and could well do so once freed from all the dogmatic certainties that have hitherto tended to surround both scripture and sacraments within the church. After all, outside of the world of religion in its narrow sense, cultic acts clearly have a genuine continuing importance. Births, birthdays, the forming of relationships, marriages, anniversaries, changes of home, changes in relationship also, retirements and finally death are just some of the occasions that human beings wish to celebrate or mark, frequently in quite formal and ritualized ways. In that sense it is true to say that there are natural rites of passage that women and men want to observe and in which, as we have noted already, they would very often wish institutionalized religion to be involved – if it could manage the grace to allow that. A liberal church will be intent on taking up these and other opportunities, and devising forms for them where they do not already exist, regardless of the cold water that conservatives are likely to want to pour upon this. There is much scope for the development of some new sacraments in a new world, such as will enable people to celebrate the significance that they intuitively sense in these life events.

But along with this, what of more traditional patterns? Historically it has been the eucharist, the mass or holy communion service in which thanks is expressed over bread and wine that are then eaten and drunk by those who worship, which has served as the regular weekly rite of passage for christians. For people who have shared in it, it has captured the worth and meaning not simply of life's turning points but of its routine, its steady and generally undramatic continuing, as well. Focusing as it does on Jesus, and on the 'night that he was betrayed', it has thus held together the real hurts of

Jesus' life, its loss and failure, in a creative tension with his followers' sense of that life's continued meaning and worth. So it has sought to do justice to that ambiguity, the horror alongside of the glory, of our human lives, to which honesty requires that we attend. Despite what christians of all traditions have at times done to it and with it, it is at heart not triumphalist but realistic. Here is a key part of its meaning for all who in one sense know themselves to be 'betrayed' in life, but who can also recognize that experience as being in fact only one area of a much broader canvas.

The eucharist thus has the capacity to be a significant sign. But the way in which it has been celebrated by the churches also presents problems for those who are open believers. First, it is plain that not all people do respond to symbols, and certainly not to symbols as ancient as these, and the extent to which any such response can ever be 'taught' is unclear. Second and more seriously perhaps, receiving holy communion has almost always been taken as an act of christian 'belonging', and as such has inevitably had the result of making others feel themselves to be 'outsiders'. Within the Church of England, as in many other denominations, the regular weekly celebration of the eucharist – the parish communion – has since the 1950s become more and more the norm for worship. If we compare the service with the dry formality of old-style Anglican mattins, there is much that has been beneficial in this, but the price paid has undoubtedly been a loss in the sense of the church's openness. For at the heart of the eucharist there does lie the taking of communion, and those who are not regular churchgoers, those who are not confirmed, cannot help but feel left out at this point where others are plainly seen to be 'in'. While it is certainly true that for the uninitiated the task of following mattins in the Book of Common Prayer was a formidable one, it was still a service that in theory at least was open to everyone. The parish communion, by contrast, has had the effect of drawing lines between 'members' and 'non-members', even though this was never intended at its inception, and to some extent at least it has helped to push the latter out. In this way it has reinforced that separating out of church from the world which it has been the whole thrust of this book to resist and to seek to reverse.

A new christianity requires a change of practice therefore which will retain the force of the eucharist's sign, but broaden the thing out so that it can become more accessible to all. Part of this need not present any real difficulty. Liberal believers should simply extend the free access they are committed to in the case of baptism to the eucharist as well. There is no reason to get hung up about the customs of the past, or to insist on great programmes of instruction before someone can take communion, or to assert the need to keep holy things holy. As with all of christianity, the eucharist is a human work, and human beings have the freedom within a living tradition to fashion the rules about it. A recast christianity will say without further fuss that there are no rules here, and that all who wish are fully welcome to share in the whole. Within the Church of England and in many other christian bodies, this already happens for those who are members of other churches. We simply broaden that out to include everybody. Most of those who take communion are probably still going to be baptized people, but not all will, nor do they need to be. Baptism – if it has not been done in infancy – can as easily and as naturally follow communion as precede it. Such a freeing of practice will also settle once and for all the agonizing over when and how children should be admitted to communion, which has been a long-running controversy within many churches. Children would be as welcome to share in communion as anyone else. So many who worship nowadays at children's or family eucharists so obviously want to, as do those who come to church regularly with their parents. They do not understand why their extended hands should not be filled like others, and many who are clergy like myself are wholly unconvinced by the reasons we are made to offer. By making real in this way a view of the eucharist as a celebration of all – and every – life, the sacrament could quite spontaneously begin to come alive for many.

Yet the effects of this alone will be limited, and some fresh thinking about the actual shape and form of the service is going to be necessary for people of a new christianity to be able to claim it for their own. Creativity is badly needed, and ought to be able to flow from our letting go of an exaggerated stress upon the 'givenness' of the service and all its ingredients. There is quite simply too much of the bible in christian worship at the present time, and as part of that far too little admitting that its writings are time-bound and culturally conditioned human works. A new christianity will want to redress the balance, setting alongside of 'scripture' a whole range – and one that is not set, but constantly changing – of other human responses to life and life's mystery, in writing, art, music and other forms. More important even than any particular ingredient itself will be the spirit, the style of its inclusion, which ought to be much more that of invitation – 'Can you see anything in this?' – than of tired and irrational authoritarian pronouncement – 'This is the Word of the Lord.'

There is also a need to root worship more genuinely in the daily experience of those who share in it: to catch more adequately the link there ought therefore to be between the thankfulness expressed, the bread eaten and the wine drunk, and the lives of those who are actually sharing in the worship. Most of the forms that get used for the central thanksgiving prayer in the service – the eucharistic prayer – put great stress upon its links with the life of Jesus (both the real and, even more, the mythical aspects of that life), but very little upon its significance for the worshippers themselves. As with so many of the other parts of the service, the emphasis is chiefly upon keeping people in order and on the rails. We see this most notoriously, perhaps, in the quite unwarranted weekly recital of a statement of fourth-century christian beliefs, the Nicene Creed, with the pretence that this is somehow an adequate expression of the faith of believers today. The combined effect of all these things together serves to give the impression that what people ought to be about is thinking the right (i.e. the historic, credal) things, rather than that they should be allowed to bring themselves, their lives and the experiences of their world now, and create worship out of this.

Any truly contemporary expression of christianity must open all this up, get away from the exclusive emphasis on the past mythic acts of an omnipotent God, and stress instead the present activity of a fallible yet creative humanity, for which Jesus serves as a type. In such a setting, the recalling of Jesus should then rekindle the hope of those for whom he matters, affirm them as themselves, and re-equip them for further life in their similar conviction that life has great worth. Actually we should avoid saying too much, or else dogmatism will re-enter by the back door. The assurance that is received from being with others who respond in similar ways to ourselves needs to be matched by an insistence on people returning to the wholeness of the wider world in which they belong, together with its untidinesses which we are not to wish away. The ingredients of the weekly christian gathering for the eucharist in the future may well change from week to week, with a variety of emphases – quietness, receiving, discussing, planning action – contributing to the whole. There are good grounds however for saying that open christians should generally content themselves with just the single weekly assembly, with an insistence at the end upon the rightness of dispersal. There is a trend nowadays among christian conservatives to assess the worth of church life in terms of its intensity, this being one more part of their distrust of the world. The more prayer groups and bible study groups there are meeting each night, the deeper must be the commitment. But any such club model needs to be firmly resisted if a genuine openness is ever going to be maintained.

Not least among the reasons for this is the fact that cultic rites, though capable of enriching and deepening our self-understanding and our self-expression, can so easily slide into superstition and, instead of liberating experiences, they are made into things to which believers are bound and upon which they become dependent. Religion has the potential to be a powerful and destructive drug, and it is to check this that it is so important always to recall and insist upon its wholly human nature. We make it and we control it, and though it can indeed work to our good we must not allow ourselves to become overtaken by it. Within conservative christianity the mechanisms and devices that allow that kind of distortion are all there. By liberals they need to be recognized, pointed to and unmasked.

One key example of this that it may be helpful to explore briefly, intimately bound up with worship, is the whole area we know as prayer, where the consequences of an open faith call for radical rethinking and clear, honest expression. In the history of christianity, prayer has been taken to complement theology. Where theology was words about God, prayer purported to be words spoken to God. But the model of God with which our time requires us to work, a model that has set aside the notion that God has given us our words about God, cannot go on pretending that. When we pray, no one is listening outside ourselves. The old picture of God as having eyes to see, ears to hear, a strong right arm to bare, we know to be just that – a symbol and an image. So in prayer, the idea of 'talking to God' and of God 'listening' and even 'responding' are equally symbolic. Actually, many traditionalists have tiptoed towards a tentative acknowledgement of this, for prayer has been held to be no less valid – and sometimes indeed been thought to be higher – when it has been done in silence or else, more recently certainly, by posture and gesture. They have not been able, however, to take the next step, admitting prayer to be a wholly human activity and none the worse for that.

John Macquarrie, though in many ways a traditional-ist in much of his theological understanding, offers words that are helpful for more liberal believers as they make that move. Prayer, he has written, is 'a fundamental style of thinking, passionate and compassionate, respon-sible and thankful, that is deeply rooted in our humanity and that manifests itself not only among believers but also among serious-minded people who do not profess any religious faith'.[2] The recognition of that common ground with others who would not see any of their activity as overtly religious is of crucial importance as we reclaim a prayer that is freed from the suspicions of magic. The heart of prayer is indeed a 'style of thinking', a way of reflecting. What we do when we pray is quite simply to bring *our* most real concerns into the context of what is for us the most really real, into the setting of what is fundamental to our life and purpose. Prayer is never at any point an alternative to human endeavour, striving, healing, forgiving or whatever. It is the placing of all such efforts and concerns within a framework that claims that they are meaningful rather than meaningless, that says that they are worthwhile and can indeed have effect. In that human, this-worldly sense, we 'bring them before God'.

Allowing that should begin to make some sort of sense of prayer for a great many people to whom all talk of supernatural appeal or intervention is repugnant both intellectually and morally. A practical illustration, of a kind familiar to many, may be helpful. A friend of mine has gone into hospital, and after he has been there a very little while I learn that he is dying. My primary concern, when he went into hospital, was with such things as that the tests he had should be thorough, the medical team skilled and professional, the nursing caring and compassionate. All these things were necessary if he was to recover and live, and no less so if he was to be comfortable when it became apparent that he was to die. Such were the *actions* that his condition required, and prayer that lays claim to being an alternative to action is a cruel lie; it is a mark of lunatic religion to dispense with blood transfusions, or vaccines, or hospital nursing on the grounds that one has got prayer instead. But prayer does sit alongside and complement such activity. When I learned that there was no medical way to save my friend's life I did not need to be told, as I was by a kindly nurse, that I might try praying. I was praying already. And my primary prayer after I knew that he was dying was no different from what it was before. It was still that if possible he should recover and live; my second prayer was that if he died it should be peaceful and comfortable.

But what is such prayer for, if it does not presume a listening God who can hear it and do something about it? It is a passionate, compassionate thinking about the matter; my articulation of what seems best and most right in a given situation, within the context of my faith in the meaning I have glimpsed within life. The prayer will not always, I hope, be what I most want *for myself*, for my perception of love and moral goodness as part of the total purpose of life should have pointed up the perils of my own selfish capacity. None the less, in the case of someone I love, my sense of life's meaning, and the possibility of this event contributing to and strengthening that meaning, both combine to suggest that the best thing is that he should recover and live. To pray for that is to say that life's meaning both seems to demand this and would be fulfilled by this. And that cannot be otherwise. To pray as a second strand that death should be peaceful and comfortable is to make a second attempt at accommodating an experience within

one's belief in the overall worth of love, given that the
first seems unlikely to be achieved. But it remains second
best, and even after his death I shall still wish that it
could have been otherwise. Whatever ways I find to
come to terms with things, it would have been better if
he had lived. Certainly we were right to channel all our
activity and enterprise to achieving that end for as long
as we could, until it became apparent that it could serve
no purpose.

In this way prayer is to be seen as part of the total
process by which as human beings we seek to make
sense of things, and fashion a response to them. We
pray because things matter to us, and we show that they
matter by our wanting also to do something about them.
Prayer is bound up with action, though the action
possible clearly differs in the case of an ill friend from
what can be done about matters on the global scene.
And of course, prayer need not only reinforce the sense
of God's purpose I have discerned already. It may change
it, as it shows the possibilities of love to be more varied
than I might have previously imagined – as it perhaps
makes it possible for me to come to terms with death as
another part of life. But this is not in any sense magic,
even though the process may very well surprise us. It is
a wholly human action within the total life of those who
belong to a community of faith. Prayer may very well
bring us to the maturity of recognizing that life's meaning
may be as fragile as a human life – which is surely close
to the heart of what we see in Jesus – yet is still not
diminished because of that. A community of people that,
through its assembly for worship, makes that sort of
realism possible for its members need not be too
apologetic about its existence.

The third justification for an open church follows
from that, and can be put more briefly. Despite the
caricatures of liberal believers that are so frequently
presented, it is realism that provides the only appropriate
basis for any vision of faith. A vision, that is, which is

something more than simply dreaming dreams and
waiting for them to happen – with the excuse for such
inactivity being the claim that they will not happen, in
any case, this side of eternity. Because open believers
are not deceived by the myths of eternity, the vision is
genuinely for the here and now. It is not to be dreamt
but created, with the local area to which the church
belongs serving as the immediate setting in which this
can be done. Liberal christian communities have placed
great stress on making real the kingdom, the common-
wealth of God in the here and now. Many liberal
believers would justify the church community – whatever
its failings and narrowness – not for itself, but primarily
as an enabler of community in its locality. It is significant
that amidst the brutality of the dogma of the free market
economy in recent years, with its exaltation of the selfish
individual and its denigration of human society, the
church has rediscovered this role of building community
outside of its own boundaries. Many local church
buildings now provide a setting for a whole range of
community activities – from baby clinics to pensioners'
parties – and so act as a focus for many who are not
personally included within their more obviously 'religious'
functions. Some of the things going on will be actively
organized by people who are church members, others
will make use of the plant with leaders from outside
those ranks, but all, one hopes, will be regarded as a
proper work of the church in translating the gospel from
theory into practice.

It would be wholly dishonest to try and claim that
things of this sort are the exclusive preserve of liberal
believers. Many traditional congregations of both
catholic and evangelical stance have also, particularly
since the publication of the report *Faith in the City*,
thrown themselves into a host of community projects of
different kinds. Yet it could be said that there exists still
a fundamental tension to their involvement in this sort
of work. The actions may say that the world and its

people matter, but the theology with which the traditionalists work still holds that conversion, rather than good works, is the core of the church's engagement with the world. So for instance Gerald Bray, in an evangelical essay on the church in which he has bemoaned the absence of God in the life of many congregations, states firmly that, 'As Christians, we need to recover our sense of spiritual purpose, and cultivate our devotional life. We should not be afraid to press these priorities in the face of people calling for more involvement in "relevant" activities of one sort or another.'[3] 'Relevant' activities, by which he presumably means the sort of social engagement we are speaking of, are for Bray not to be understood as being properly any part of the spiritual, and can pose a threat to the church's devotional purpose.

People who are not churchgoers pick up the vibrations of this. They sense that the kindness and generosity that may well be being shown them is none the less two-edged: that it conceals a hidden agenda of wanting to bring them into the sheep-fold. They may not mind this if the club or facilities on offer suit their needs, but they feel the lack of integrity and consistency in what is going on – not least if the mother at the church-housed baby clinic discovers that her child is not made welcome within the same four walls when it comes to its being christened – and make a mental note that church people are as devious in their ways as politicians.

A reformed christianity can and must renounce this and clear the air. Working with and for people so that their humanity can be fulfilled is not a means to an end, but is the church's whole purpose. We are not in the business of recruiting for heaven, but of celebrating and renewing the here and now, and lives and people within it. That, in reality, is what the christian community is here for. We need to say this plainly, and to share the task with as many as possible of those other people for whom it also matters.

8

Sufficient for the day

We have charted the outline of what a new christianity might be like. It is not new in the sense that it wants to jettison the whole of the past – whatever accusations conservatives may be quick to make. But it is radically recast because of its determination to take the present day and its realities, as best we can see and understand them, as the starting off point, the basic given by which that tradition has always to be judged, rather than the reverse. Of necessity it is only an outline, to which the experience of a community living faith in this way will go on adding more the whole time. Yet even in so provisional a form it clearly raises certain basic questions, which must be met and answered before we finish.

The first, and almost certainly the one that is going to be put most insistently, will be 'Is this still christianity?' It is the question that is bound to be asked by those who as members of the churches are happy and content with the faith they have, and who really cannot recognize this strange growth we have been exploring, with its claim to be the heir to what is so dear to them. And clearly there is justice in their asking this. For in any number of respects we have moved a world away from the ancient faith that it seemed perfectly possible and wholly natural to express in terms of creeds and doctrines. The idea of christianity as something given, of a body of belief that could be handed down from one generation to the next, and that, with a few minor adjustments of detail, would go on making perfect sense – this concept has gone completely. We are not wanting to say merely that a

111

particular old version of faith does not any longer
command such authority. We are stressing the necessity
of taking on board the fact that no version can ever do so
again. But assurance and timelessness, our questioners
will want to insist, are part and parcel not just of
christianity, but of virtually any tradition of faith. If we
are determined to play things so differently now, surely
it would be less confusing and also more honest to face
this fact squarely, and give to what we have created a
new name instead?

Yet however plausible that may sound, the desire to
distinguish is too simple. Honest inspection of the
christian past reveals not timelessness but a constant
flux, as words take on new meanings and emphases
shift and turn, adapting to different times, settings and
peoples. Traditionalists prefer, however, to draw a veil
over this process, while in our own day it is easily lost
sight of simply because we are part of it. So while we
agree that the changes to which these objectors point are
real enough, they ought to be recognized as actually no
greater than those that are involved when anyone
nowadays utters first- or fourth-century formulations of
faith in the twentieth century, and is honest enough
then to compare their way of using these words with the
original use in the past. Our open christianity is just as
much christianity today as any of these other and
allegedly older versions so anxious to claim the title of
orthodoxy. It is christianity because its inspiration
remains Jesus, together with everything that has flowed
from him down the intervening centuries. The portrait
of Jesus is enlarged, to be sure, and the particular
stresses within it are different at several points from
those that counted for most with the people who
followed him first. It would be better, however, to
acknowledge with grace that these are the inevitable
consequences of the passage of time than to go on
regretting them as a falling away from historic truth.
Jesus' life could not help but be enlarged as it became

the common property of others, and as it was passed on to people whose experiences, circumstances and settings were quite different from his own.

Indeed, we would put it more strongly than that. The survival of that life as the inspiration of a living community required that this should happen, for we cannot all pretend that we are wandering Galilean preachers during the Roman occupation of Palestine, any more than we can claim to share every detail of the worldview that Jesus' time and place instilled in him. Ever since St Paul first spoke of the christian community as being 'the body of Christ', believers have in fact acknowledged that the life of Jesus is something that is constantly expanding to take in the lives of those who look to him. But the new strands and strains that enter the picture need to be seen not as threats to his influence but as enriching and renewing for it. Borrowing an image from the biological sciences, we should think creatively of the emergence of new genes so that the species can adjust to new circumstances, rather than be worrying the whole time about the threat of the original being lost or obliterated. Better, surely, to recognize that its survival actually requires the new.

A second question will not be heard so loudly, if only because those who ask it are most likely to be people outside the structures of religion and probably unconcerned about what seem to them to be its private, domestic quarrels. That is no reason, however, for disregarding it or its force. It would be the question, 'Is this version of faith really any more "of this world" than the old orthodoxies?' In other words, for all the attempt to start from how life is and where people are, does this alleged freeing of religious faith actually do justice to or touch the most basic concern – which would be the constant struggle simply for survival – of so many of the people of our planet?

When I turn on my television and see the sickening realities of hardship for both the young and old in vast areas of Africa, or the Indian sub-continent, or South America, when I am shown their poverty, starvation and disease, and a life constantly preoccupied with the hunt for the bare necessities of food and shelter, questions like these must carry great weight. If I allow myself to acknowledge the part of religion in the maintenance of these injustices, and that of christianity quite as much as any more 'primitive' patterns of belief (witness the effects on parents and children in the Third World of Roman Catholicism's prohibiting of contraception), they become that much more insistent. I cannot but wonder whether all that has been argued here might not become just another layer of fantasy, less morally repugnant perhaps than some of what religion has been up to before, but no less likely to distract people from tackling reality.

Nor is it only the Third World experience that prompts such questioning. British life may not appear to have quite these extremes of misery, but there are other problems that are just as real to those caught up in them – and perhaps in some ways even more real since they have to be borne in the face of others' affluence and comfort. It is all right for me to speak about life's meaning – I can afford an annual holiday and go out when I want to for a meal, or enjoy an evening at the theatre and take a taxi home afterwards, or decide to sit quietly at home and listen to a new CD. But what about so many of my fellow human beings?

I have only to think of some of the people I meet in Cambridge where I live: this city that is so beautiful in its public face with the university and colleges, and a booming city in financial terms, being in the second-fastest growing region of Britain. I can think of a teenage mother with a baby. Abandoned by her partner in the house just made available to them by the council, but not before he had wrecked the few pieces of furniture they had been given. The sheets tacked up over the windows now hide from view the sofa that has been slashed and the bedding burnt on the fire. Or another young couple, this time staying together, but the wife able to do very little because of recurrent mental and physical ill health. The husband therefore has to look after the children and home, does just occasional evening work, and is constantly having to check his pocket as he deals with the rent and the other bills and sees what is left for the family's food. They are frowned on by some of their neighbours, who resent what to them seems ineptitude and the resultant lowering of the tone of the area; but this couple are at least fortunate in having support from one another and their families. Many others are not so lucky. Or there is an older, single man, who has worked hard all his life at a series of very ordinary jobs, cared for sick parents, never earned a lot, and has certainly never been in a position to benefit from any contributory pension scheme. His mother and father are now both dead, and he struggles to survive on his own in their council flat with his state pension. With nothing to show in the way of possessions for a working life, he tries to relax in front of the bulky old black and white television set, but is at his wits' end as rents rise to become 'realistic' in accord with government policy. Further limited by his own increasing disabilities, he finally fails to meet new water charges, and receives a summons. An old friend bails him out, and he swallows his strongly independent pride and allows this, only to receive one further humiliating swipe – a bill from the water company for 'legal costs'.

And I could think of many others. Where life is such a constant struggle, is not our religious claim for meaning a jest, well meaning no doubt, on the part of those who do not know the way things truly are? Yet in fact two of these people I have mentioned – or their slightly veiled originals – have wanted to involve the church in some way in working through these experiences, refusing to be defeated by them, while the third has allowed some offer of practical assistance. Honest and open religion is not pretending that life is not a struggle for many, nor is it content that things remain like that. It is for this very reason that a new christianity cannot but be 'political', if politics is what we choose to call a determined longing to move forward the way things are in this one life that is ours. What such faith does refuse to accept is that life is always bound to be this struggle. So it seeks ways for making change real. There is a genuine earthing to this, a realistic this-worldliness. Open christians are not in the business of offering bliss once this life is past, as in Charles Wesley's dreary dirge –

> Hide me, O my Saviour, hide,
> Till the storm of life is past;
> Safe into the haven guide;
> O receive my soul at last!

– but of making *this* world what it ought to be.

On which basis, the view of religious faith we are suggesting might even be held to be more this-worldly not only than much traditional religion, but also much conventional politics as well. Party politicians can become so committed to their particular vision of the future that the present moment almost has to be discounted by them. When I have dealings as a parish priest with local politicians in both the main parties, I quite often seem to meet with an almost ideological refusal to acknowledge any possibility of good in any situation for which the other side exercises responsibility. Worth and meaning have no place here, but can only lie ahead, in a future to which they alone possess the key. There is a weird sense of *déjà vu* in the parallel between this and so many encounters with the conventionally religious. The open christian, by contrast, will want to insist on the importance of the here and now, with the conviction, borrowing some ancient words of Irenaeus, that 'the glory of God is a living human being' and that this is the basis of working to change the world – change that may show more clearly the way things actually are. In the light of the continuing story of Jesus, worth and meaning are the possession of everyone right now. These assets are not to be understood as the preserve of the 'successful', not even that version of success alleged as accessible in an idyllic future to all who sign on the correct dotted line of faith. In one sense, to be sure, reflection in this way on the meaning of life is always going to be a luxury. Yet it is a luxury to which women and men have entitlement, and one that is fully justified when linked to action to give substance to what is believed.

The final key question that requires a response is one that will probably be the open believer's own. It is, quite simply, 'Is it worth it?' It is a question that is likely to be prompted not so much by any personal anxiety about the appropriateness of an open faith, but more on account of the lack of sympathy, and sometimes downright hostility, shown towards such a faith by those most eager to call themselves christians. A couple of sentences from a letter I once received from a Unitarian minister catch a dimension to life within mainstream christianity that many others will know. 'You are brave to use the word "liberal". I thought never again in my life-time to see this word used non-opprobriously by an Anglican parson.' Plenty of open believers within the life of the church, and plenty more outside who would welcome just such a credible faith, will identify with how those words strike home. These are not easy times in which to express this way of believing. The emphasis of the public spokesmen of the churches is all on certainty and assurance, despite the many underlying insecurities within that have surely given rise to this. George Carey, the Archbishop of Canterbury, is anxious to stress this in so many of his public statements. 'There is a new confidence abroad in our church; the sap is rising and new life flowing through the body.'[1] Many who pursue that line are very unwilling to let the public broad grin be challenged by any indication of liberal hesitancy.

Rather than despair at such circumstances, though, what open believers have to do is discover a proper confidence of their own. It will certainly be distinguished from the prevailing cult of answers and of certainties, and it will need to emphasize the worth of hesitancy, the value of the non-dogmatic, and the fact that these are actually quite different from mere indecision. I have quoted Maurice Wiles more than once. Some further words of his seem to strike the right note in providing appropriate foundations for confidence in a christianity set free along these lines:

> The position in which we find ourselves is one which seems to call at the same time *for an absoluteness of commitment and a recognition of the limitation of our own perspective*, both as individuals and as the Christian community. Do without the first and there is a crippling loss of religious vitality; do without the second and there is a danger not merely of absolutizing our own perspective but of religious fanaticism as well.[2]

If the perils of failing to recognize 'the limitation of our own perspective' are all too clear to liberals now in the climate of a new religious fanaticism which has become even more apparent during the ten years since Wiles wrote, the duty of making plain a corresponding 'absoluteness of commitment' surely becomes that much more urgent. It does not mean that we must pretend that everything in the garden is lovely. But it does mean overcoming those anxieties about our right to be here, authentically part of the whole christian movement, which we have too easily allowed traditionalists to wish upon us. Living with doubts and questioning, far from being an undermining of the way of faith and requiring apology, needs to be stated much more clearly as being right at the heart of that way. Tradition (and the bible as part of that tradition) offers the story of a faith community to people in the contemporary world, but it can never do more than hint at what that present should now be doing with that story. The key to owning the past lies in admitting first of all that it is past. Only when that is done, and when the unique reality and absolute importance of the present moment has been fully taken on board, can we use that past in ways that are imaginative and creative, rather than restrictive and limiting.

Part of the freedom this offers, I suggest, is in fact a freedom to cope with the conservatives and not be overwhelmed. The intolerance and credulousness that we see in them is itself woven into the story we inherit at many points, as it is into those of just about every other tradition of faith. If that disturbs by making plain that this conflict is not something that we are going to avoid, it should also reassure with its reminder that things do still move on. The world is not, in fact, constrained by the church's obscurantism for long, and in the struggles between new knowledge and religious conservatism the outcome is not in doubt. Those who are open to the world's insights, those responsive to both the present moment and its future promise, are the ones who determine a new pattern, whatever short-term disapproval they may face. And even that disapproval is matched by the gratitude of others. They may well be people who keep outside the world of formal religion, but they are people grateful that this dimension of worth to life is not lost by being abandoned to obsolete worldviews. That sympathy is much more important to open believers than any amount of name-calling by the 'orthodox', and it is on such sympathizers that attention from now on should focus. A non-dogmatic commitment along these lines both affirms that life matters now, and should also help to keep alive that possibility, and 'the rumour of God', for those who follow later.

Those who do follow are of course not going to see everything as we do today. The pattern we have suggested is itself as time-bound and provisional as all the others that have preceded it. We cannot pretend that we are laying down fresh laws of the Medes and Persians, and liberal confidence must not be allowed to become liberal dogmatism – that would be a sad irony indeed! New knowledge and fresh understandings of humanity and the world will change this version of faith as they always have done in the past. The only difference is likely to be the speed with which this will happen, given the pace of change in everything else. The mould will need to be cracked time and again as faith learns to be regularly recast in the light of new realities.

Allowing there to be room for that is central to the whole style of believing that has been explored here. All too often the church's response to new worlds has appeared reluctant and grudging, and a matter of conceding the minimum of change necessary so that old ways can limp on a little more. Inevitably this has resulted in a 'God of the gaps', steadily shrinking away, yet with her followers desperately trying to cling on to a range of titles and attributes long after these have been robbed of any genuine substance. Christian faith has thus become just another nostalgia industry – at one level, to be sure, booming with the rest of them, but wholly divorced from where people are living now. If that is part of its charm for those within the traditional churches' folds, it is also the clinching proof of its irrelevance to all the people who are not.

Finding a way forward from here demands that we now recognize that God too has to change, if what God represents is ever going to be made available to future generations. Though in one sense, indeed, we can only live in our present moment, we surely owe it to those who follow us to take that future very seriously. That involves acknowledging the full extent of our human responsibility for creating faith, as well as for the world of which faith is a part. The task, which has occupied us throughout these pages, is quite simply to realize the desire and longing to save God, a God which matters, for that world. If the future for faith does run out, it will only be because that has been dismissed as unfaith.

Notes

Introduction

1. D. E. Nineham, 'The Use of the Bible in Modern Theology', in *Explorations in Theology 1* (SCM Press 1977), p. 111.

1 The failure of christian orthodoxy

1. 'How lovely on the mountains are the feet of Him', words by L. E. Smith Jnr, © 1974/1978 Thank You Music, included in *Mission Praise* (Marshall, Morgan & Scott 1983).
2. 'Those who love and those who labour follow in the way of Christ', words by Geoffrey Dearmer, included in *Songs of Praise* (Oxford University Press 1925).
3. For much more on the changes in current Anglican practice, and the dangers of alienation that result from it, see M. Dalby, *Open Baptism* (SPCK 1989).
4. The phrase 'ritual purity' I owe to Mary Douglas, though its particular use here is my own. Her *Natural Symbols* (Penguin 1973) has a great deal that is of interest and relevance on the abdication by religion of its responsibility for a society's ritual.
5. See, for instance, *Faith in the City* (Church House Publishing 1985), chapter 4 in particular, and also *Faith in the Countryside* (Churchman Publishing 1990), both of which stress the importance of a church congregation's commitment to the wider local community of which it forms a part.
6. A useful overview of the nineteenth century is provided in J. Walvin, *Victorian Values* (André Deutsch 1987).
7. See on this, A. Hastings, *A History of English Christianity, 1920–1990* (third edn, SCM Press 1991), chapter 40, pp. 630ff.

8. For the sermons, see D. E. Jenkins, *God, Jesus and Life in the Spirit* (SCM Press 1988), pp. 105–21.
9. H. Dawes, 'Liberal Christianity in the Parish: A Lost Cause?', *Theology*, March/April 1990, pp. 117–24.
10. W. Meeks, *The Moral World of the First Christians* (SPCK 1987), p. 13.
11. ibid.
12. T. S. Eliot, 'Little Gidding' from *Four Quartets*, in *Collected Poems 1909–1962* (Faber & Faber 1963), p. 220.

2 *A new story of God*

1. J. I. Packer, 'Understanding the Bible: Evangelical Hermeneutics', in M. Tinker (ed.), *Restoring the Vision – Anglican Evangelicals Speak Out* (Monarch 1990), p. 50.
2. G. Tyrrell, *Through Scylla and Charybdis* (London 1907), p. 281.
3. N. Sagovsky's *'On God's Side' – A Life of George Tyrrell* (OUP 1990) is a splendid study of both the life and work of Tyrrell. J. H. S. Kent's *The End of the Line? – The Development of Christian Theology in the Last Two Centuries* (SCM Press 1982) provides a valuable, albeit painful, introduction to the struggles in the period between conservatives and liberals.
4. 1 Corinthians 3.19.
5. *Chance and Necessity* – the title of a book by Jacques Monod (Eng. tr. Collins 1972).
6. R. Swinburne, *The Coherence of Theism* (Clarendon Press 1977), p. 1. I owe it to Don Cupitt's *Life Lines* (SCM Press 1986) for drawing my attention to Swinburne's definition.
7. See Acts 17.16ff.
8. For a beautiful and finely wrought instance of this approach, but one still ultimately inadequate, see W. H. Vanstone, *Love's Endeavour, Love's Expense* (Darton, Longman & Todd 1977).
9. Acts 1.11.
10. 'Saboteur of received ideas' from William Plomer's 'A Church in Bavaria' in *Collected Poems* (Jonathan Cape 1973), pp. 256ff.

11. In ibid., pp. 223ff.
12. P. Larkin, 'Church Going', in *The Less Deceived* (The Marvell Press 1955), pp. 28ff.

3 *The worth of humanity*

 1. C. Wright, 'Inter-Faith Dialogue and the Uniqueness of Christ', in Tinker (ed.), *Restoring the Vision*, p. 107.
 2. Told by A. E. Harvey in *Francis Hugh Maycock: A Tribute* (S.L.G.Press 1981).
 3. M. Tinker, 'Content, Context and Culture: Proclaiming the Gospel Today', in Tinker (ed.), *Restoring the Vision*, p. 68.
 4. ibid., p. 79.
 5. A. McGrath, *Doubt: Handling it Honestly* (Inter-Varsity Press 1990), p. 143.
 6. D. Holloway, *A Nation under God* (Kingsway Publications 1987), p. 124.
 7. ibid., p. 126.
 8. 'Moral fragility'. I owe the phrase, along with much else, to Professor Leslie Houlden; see *Truth Untold: Meditations on the Gospel* (SPCK 1991), pp. 43ff.
 9. M. Wiles, 'Does Christology Rest on a Mistake?', in *Working Papers in Doctrine* (SCM Press 1976), p. 127.
10. *The Myth of God Incarnate*. I borrow the title of a book that caused some stir when it first appeared, earning all sorts of censure from traditionalists, yet which can now be seen to have given expression to the actual beliefs of a considerable number of christians, and to the gut feelings of the great majority of people outside the church (J. Hick, ed., SCM Press 1977).
11. Geoffrey Lampe, essay in *Christian Believing: The Nature of the Christian Faith and its Expression in Holy Scripture and the Creeds*, The Doctrine Commission of the Church of England (SPCK 1976), p. 111. The effective losing of the report in the synodical processes of the Church of England says a great deal about how conservative believers react to open christian insight.
12. C. Wright, *What's so Unique about Jesus* (Monarch 1990).

13. ibid., p. 58.
14. J. Bowden, *Jesus: The Unanswered Questions* (SCM Press 1988), p. 207.

4 Faith in life

1. N. Anderson, *Jesus Christ; the Witness of History* (Inter-Varsity Press 1985), p. 18.
2. D. MacKinnon, 'Order and Evil in the Gospel', in *Borderlands of Theology and other Essays* (Lutterworth Press 1968), p. 95.
3. See in particular Alfred Loisy's *L'Évangile et L'Église* (Paris 1902, E.T. *The Gospel and the Church*, London 1903), which remains full of illuminating insight.
4. D. Jenkins, Easter sermon for 1987, in *God, Jesus and Life in the Spirit* (SCM Press 1988), p. 115.
5. G. Lampe, 'The Essence of Christianity', in *Explorations in Theology 8* (SCM Press 1981), p. 128.
6. *The Rural Church Project: The Views of Rural Parishioners* (Dept of Theology, University of Nottingham 1990), reported in *The Times*, 22 September 1990.
7. Easter sermon for 1988, Jenkins, p. 118.
8. J. A. T. Robinson, 'Evil and the God of Love', in *Where Three Ways Meet* (SCM Press 1987), p. 185.
9. G. Lampe, 'Mere Sermon, Preparation for Death', in *Explorations in Theology 8*, pp. 133ff.

5 Renewing the world

1. D. Holloway, *A Nation under God* (Kingsway Publications 1987), p. 177.
2. See, for instance, as a guide to the conservative view, P. Moore (ed.), *Man, Woman and Priesthood* (SPCK 1978). For an introduction to the call for change, see M. Furlong (ed.), *Feminine in the Church* (SPCK 1984). And for a very forceful statement of the impossibility of any view still bound by the past, see D. Hampson, *Theology and Feminism* (Basil Blackwell 1990).
3. Hampson, *Theology and Feminism*, p. 88.
4. ibid. Hampson is very clear on this matter of the radical discontinuity between past and present. See pp. 41ff.

6 *Valuing what is ordinary*

1. M. Wiles, *The Remaking of Christian Doctrine* (SCM Press 1974), p. 115.
2. T. Walker, 'As the Spirit Wills: Evangelicals, the Charismatic Movement and the Church of England', in Tinker (ed.), *Restoring the Vision*, p. 179.
3. G. Angel, *Delusion or Dynamite? Reflections on a quarter century of Charismatic Renewal* (Monarch 1989), p. 114.
4. A. N. Wilson, *Against Religion: Why We Should Try to Live Without It* (Chatto & Windus 1991), pp. 18ff.
5. ibid., p. 19.
6. See J. Hick, 'The Non-Absoluteness of Christianity', in J. Hick and P. F. Knitter (eds), *The Myth of Christian Uniqueness* (SCM Press 1987).
7. From 'Reinventing the Human'. An interview with Thomas Berry by Mark Matousek, published in *Leading Edge*, Summer 1991.
8. ibid.
9. P. White, *The Solid Mandala* (Eyre and Spottiswoode 1966).

7 *An open church*

1. Wilson, *Against Religion*, p. 45.
2. J. Macquarrie, *Paths in Spirituality* (SCM Press 1972), p. 30. (I owe the quotation to its use in an article by Derek Webster in *Theology*, July/August 1991).
3. G. Bray, 'What is the Church? An Ecclesiology for Today', in Tinker (ed.), *Restoring the Vision*, p. 201.

8 *Sufficient for the day*

1. G. Carey, 'Ecclesiology and Mission – Implications for Church Planting', address to Church Planting Conference, 22 May 1991.
2. M. Wiles, *Faith and the Mystery of God* (SCM Press 1982), p. 4, my italics.

Index

abortion 73-4
Acts, book of 29
Anderson, N. 54-5, 125
Angel, G. 86, 126
Auden, W. H. 62

Baelz, P. 50
baptism of infants 12-13
Barth, K. 26-7
Berry, T. 94-5, 126
bible 22, 24-5, 71-3, 103
Bowden, J. 53, 125
Bray, G. 110, 126

Calvin, J. 7
Carey, G. 117-18, 126
Cupitt, D. 123

Dalby, M. 122
David, King 25, 30
Dawes, H. W. 123
Dearmer, G. 8, 122
Dearmer, P. 8
death 63-6
Doctrine Commission 49, 124
Douglas, M. 122

Eliot, T. S. 123
Eluard, P. 95

environmentalism 70, 81, 93-5
ethics: christian response to changes in 15; provisionality of 75-82
eucharist 100-5
evangelism: decade of 6, 39-40, 98; as propaganda 74-5
exclusivism, christian 2, 11-15, 35, 57, 96; setting aside of 91-3

Faith in the City 109, 122
Faith in the Countryside 122
Furlong, M. 125

Genesis myths 38, 42-4, 78, 93
Gummer, J. 1-2

Hampson, D. 78, 125
Harvey, A. E. 124
Hebrews, letter to the 66
Hick, J. 65, 92, 124, 126
Holloway, D. 41-2, 70, 124-5
Houlden, J. L. 124
hymns: failings of modern 7-8

incarnation myth 49-50, 83-4
islam 10, 96
Irenaeus 116

Jenkins, D. E. 16, 55, 59-61, 123, 125
Jesus: type for humanity 29, 31, 45-53, 104; and ethics 72-7, 81; and women 78, 80; death of 8, 46, 57-8, 108; resurrection of 16, 54-61, 66-7; his enlarging portrait 112-13
John, gospel of 4, 46, 58, 76, 95
John Paul II, pope 16
judaism 21, 29-31, 38, 71-2, 78

Kent, J. H. S. 123

Lampe, G. W. H. 49-50, 59-60, 65, 124-5
Larkin, P. 36, 124
legal codes, religious 71-5
Loisy, A. 125

McGrath, A. 41, 124
MacKinnon, D. M. 56-7, 125
Macquarrie, J. 106, 126
Mark, gospel of 53, 56-7, 73
Matthew, gospel of 74, 76
Maycock, H. 40, 124
Meeks, W. 18, 123
misery, human 113-16

Modernism, Roman Catholic 1, 25-6, 58
Monod, J. 123
Moore, P. 125
moral fragility 38-45, 90-1
Moses 25

New Age 94
Newman, J. H. 25
Nineham, D. E. 3, 122

Packer, J. I. 22, 123
parish system 14
Paul the apostle 18, 27, 29, 39, 43, 45, 54-6, 79, 113
Pilate, Pontius 4
Pius X, pope 1, 26
Plomer, W. 33-4, 123
prayer 28-9, 105-8

Quakers 49

resurrection 61-7
revelation 21-7
Robinson, J. A. T. 63, 125
Rushdie, S. 10

Sagovsky, N. 123
sin *see* moral fragility
Songs of Praise 8, 122
supernaturalism 29-31, 85-90
Swinburne, R. 28, 123

Third World 81, 93, 114

Tillich, P. 25
Tinker, M. 40, 123-4, 125
Tyrrell, G. 25-6, 123

Vanstone, W. H. 123

Walker, A. 41
Walker, T. 86, 126
Walvin, J. 122

Wesley, C. 116
White, P. 95, 126
Wiles, M. 48, 73-4, 118, 124, 126
Wilson, A. N. 89, 97, 126
women: church subjugation of 77-81
World Development Movement 69
Wright, C. 39, 51, 124-5